The Faerie Queene by Edmund Spenser

Book III. The Legend of Britomartis

THE THIRDE BOOKE OF THE FAERIE QUEENE CONTAYNING THE LEGEND OF BRITOMARTIS OR OF CHASTITY

One of the greatest of English poets, Edmund Spenser was born in East Smithfield, London, in 1552. He was educated in London at the Merchant Taylors' School and later at Pembroke College, Cambridge. In 1579, he published The Shepheardes Calender, his first major work.

Edmund journeyed to Ireland in July 1580, in the service of the newly appointed Lord Deputy, Arthur Grey, 14th Baron Grey de Wilton. His time included the terrible massacre at the Siege of Smerwick.

The epic poem, The Faerie Queene, is acknowledged as Edmund's masterpiece. The first three books were published in 1590, and a second set of three books were published in 1596.

Indeed the reality is that Spenser, through his great talents, was able to move Poetry in a different direction. It led to him being called a Poet's Poet and brought rich admiration from Milton, Raleigh, Blake, Wordsworth, Keats, Byron, and Lord Tennyson, among others.

Spenser returned to Ireland and in 1591, Complaints, a collection of poems that voices complaints in mournful or mocking tones was published.

In 1595, Spenser published Amoretti and Epithalamion. The volume contains eighty-nine sonnets.

In the following year Spenser wrote a prose pamphlet titled A View of the Present State of Ireland, a highly inflammatory argument for the pacification and destruction of Irish culture.

On January 13th 1599 Edmund Spenser died at the age of forty-six. His coffin was carried to his grave in Westminster Abbey by other poets, who threw many pens and pieces of poetry into his grave followed with many tears.

Index of Contents
Book III. The Legend of Britomartis
Introductory Verses
Canto I
Canto II
Canto III
Canto IV
Canto V
Canto VI
Canto VII
Canto VIII
Canto IX
Canto X
Canto XI
Canto XII
Edmund Spenser – A Short Biography

Edmund Spenser – A Concise Bibliography

INTRODUCTORY VERSES

I
It falls me here to write of Chastity,
That fayrest vertue, far above the rest;
For which what needes me fetch from Faery
Forreine ensamples, it to have exprest?
Sith it is shrined in my Soveraines brest,
And formd so lively in each perfect part,
That to all ladies, which have it profest,
Neede but behold the pourtraict of her hart,
If pourtrayd it might bee by any living art.

II
But living art may not least part expresse,
Nor life-resembling pencill it can paynt,
All were it Zeuxis or Praxiteles:
His dædale hand would faile, and greatly faynt,
And her perfections with his error taynt:
Ne poets witt, that passeth painter farre
In picturing the parts of beauty daynt,
So hard a workemanship adventure darre,
For fear through want of words her excellence to marre.

III
How then shall I, apprentice of the skill
That whilome in divinest wits did rayne,
Presume so high to stretch mine humble quill?
Yet now my luckelesse lott doth me constrayne
Hereto perforce. But, O dredd Soverayne,
Thus far forth pardon, sith that choicest witt
Cannot your glorious pourtraict figure playne,
That I in colour showes may shadow itt,
And antique praises unto present persons fitt.

IV
But if in living colours, and right hew,
Your selfe you covet to see pictured,
Who can it doe more lively, or more trew,
Then that sweete verse, with nectar sprinckeled,
In which a gracious servaunt pictured
His Cynthia, his heavens fayrest light?
That with his melting sweetnes ravished,
And with the wonder of her beames bright,
My sences lulled are in slomber of delight.

V

But let that same delitious poet lend
A little leave unto a rusticke Muse
To sing his mistresse prayse, and let him mend,
If ought amis her liking may abuse:
Ne let his fayrest Cynthia refuse,
In mirrours more then one her selfe to see,
But either Gloriana let her chuse,
Or in Belphœbe fashioned to bee:
In th' one her rule, in th' other her rare chastitee.

CANTO I

Guyon encountreth Britomart:
Fayre Florimell is chaced:
Duessaes traines and Malecastaes
Champions are defaced.

I
The famous Briton Prince and Faery knight,
After long wayes and perilous paines endur'd,
Having their weary limbes to perfect plight
Restord, and sory wounds right well recur'd,
Of the faire Alma greatly were procur'd
To make there lenger sojourne and abode;
But when thereto they might not be allur'd
From seeking praise and deeds of armes abrode,
They courteous conge tooke, and forth together yode.

II
But the captiv'd Acrasia he sent,
Because of traveill long, a nigher way,
With a strong gard, all reskew to prevent,
And her to Faery court safe to convay,
That her for witnes of his hard assay
Unto his Faery Queene he might present:
But he him selfe betooke another way,
To make more triall of his hardiment,
And seeke adventures, as he with Prince Arthure went.

III
Long so they traveiled through wastefull wayes,
Where daungers dwelt, and perils most did wonne,
To hunt for glory and renowmed prayse:
Full many countreyes they did overronne,
From the uprising to the setting sunne,
And many hard adventures did atchieve;
Of all the which they honour ever wonne,

Seeking the weake oppressed to relieve,
And to recover right for such as wrong did grieve.

IV
At last, as through an open plaine they yode,
They spide a knight, that towards pricked fayre;
And him beside an aged squire there rode,
That seemd to couch under his shield three-square,
As if that age badd him that burden spare,
And yield it those that stouter could it wield:
He them espying, gan him selfe prepare,
And on his arme addresse his goodly shield,
That bore a lion passant in a golden field.

V
Which seeing good Sir Guyon, deare besought
The Prince, of grace, to let him ronne that turne.
He graunted: then the Faery quickly raught
His poynant speare, and sharply gan to spurne
His fomy steed, whose fiery feete did burne
The verdant gras, as he thereon did tread;
Ne did the other backe his foote returne,
But fiercely forward came withouten dread,
And bent his dreadful speare against the others head.

VI
They beene ymett, and both theyr points arriv'd;
But Guyon drove so furious and fell,
That seemd both shield and plate it would have riv'd:
Nathelesse it bore his foe not from his sell,
But made him stagger, as he were not well:
But Guyon selfe, ere well he was aware,
Nigh a speares length behind his crouper fell;
Yet in his fall so well him selfe he bare,
That mischievous mischaunce his life and limbs did spare.

VII
Great shame and sorrow of that fall he tooke;
For never yet, sith warlike armes he bore,
And shivering speare in bloody field first shooke,
He fownd him selfe dishonored so sore.
Ah! gentlest knight that ever armor bore,
Let not thee grieve dismounted to have beene,
And brought to grownd, that never wast before;
For not thy fault, but secret powre unseene:
That speare enchaunted was, which layd thee on the greene.

VIII
But weenedst thou what wight thee overthrew,
Much greater griefe and shamefuller regrett
For thy hard fortune then thou wouldst renew,

That of a single damzell thou wert mett
On equall plaine, and there so hard besett:
Even the famous Britomart it was,
Whom straunge adventure did from Britayne fett,
To seeke her lover, (love far sought, alas!)
Whose image shee had seene in Venus looking glas.

IX
Full of disdainefull wrath, he fierce uprose,
For to revenge that fowle reprochefull shame,
And snatching his bright sword, began to close
With her on foot, and stoutly forward came;
Dye rather would he then endure that same.
Which when his palmer saw, he gan to feare
His toward perill and untoward blame,
Which by that new rencounter he should reare:
For death sate on the point of that enchaunted speare.

X
And hasting towards him gan fayre perswade,
Not to provoke misfortune, nor to weene
His speares default to mend with cruell blade:
For by his mightie science he had seene
The secrete vertue of that weapon keene,
That mortall puissaunce mote not withstond:
Nothing on earth mote alwaies happy beene.
Great hazard were it, and adventure fond,
To loose long gotten honour with one evill hond.

XI
By such good meanes he him discounselled
From prosecuting his revenging rage;
And eke the Prince like treaty handeled,
His wrathfull will with reason to aswage,
And laid the blame, not to his carriage,
But to his starting steed, that swarv'd asyde,
And to the ill purveyaunce of his page,
That had his furnitures not firmely tyde:
So is his angry corage fayrly pacifyde.

XII
Thus reconcilement was betweene them knitt,
Through goodly temperaunce and affection chaste;
And either vowd with all their power and witt,
To let not others honour be defaste
Of friend or foe, who ever it embaste,
Ne armes to beare against the others syde:
In which accord the Prince was also plaste,
And with that golden chaine of concord tyde.
So goodly all agreed, they forth yfere did ryde.

XIII
O goodly usage of those antique tymes,
In which the sword was servaunt unto right!
When not for malice and contentious crymes,
But all for prayse, and proofe of manly might,
The martiall brood accustomed to fight:
Then honour was the meed of victory,
And yet the vanquished had no despight:
Let later age that noble use envy,
Vyle rancor to avoid, and cruel surquedry.

XIV
Long they thus traveiled in friendly wise,
Through countreyes waste and eke well edifyde,
Seeking adventures hard, to exercise
Their puissaunce, whylome full dernly tryde:
At length they came into a forest wyde,
Whose hideous horror and sad trembling sownd
Full griesly seemd: therein they long did ryde,
Yet tract of living creature none they fownd,
Save beares, lyons, and buls, which romed them arownd.

XV
All suddenly out of the thickest brush,
Upon a milkwhite palfrey all alone,
A goodly lady did foreby them rush,
Whose face did seeme as cleare as christall stone,
And eke through feare as white as whales bone:
Her garments all were wrought of beaten gold,
And all her steed with tinsell trappings shone,
Which fledd so fast that nothing mote him hold,
And scarse them leasure gave, her passing to behold.

XVI
Still as she fledd her eye she backward threw,
As fearing evill that poursewd her fast;
And her faire yellow locks behind her flew,
Loosely disperst with puff of every blast:
All as a blazing starre doth farre outcast
His hearie beames, and flaming lockes dispredd,
At sight whereof the people stand aghast:
But the sage wisard telles, as he has redd,
That it importunes death and dolefull dreryhedd.

XVII
So as they gazed after her a whyle,
Lo! where a griesly foster forth did rush,
Breathing out beastly lust her to defyle:
His tyreling jade he fiersly forth did push,
Through thicke and thin, both over banck and bush,
In hope her to attaine by hooke or crooke,

That from his gory sydes the blood did gush:
Large were his limbes, and terrible his looke,
And in his clownish hand a sharp bore speare he shooke.

XVIII
Which outrage when those gentle knights did see,
Full of great envy and fell gealosy,
They stayd not to avise who first should bee,
But all spurd after fast as they mote fly,
To reskew her from shamefull villany.
The Prince and Guyon equally bylive
Her selfe pursewd, in hope to win thereby
Most goodly meede, the fairest dame alive:
But after the foule foster Timias did strive.

XIX
The whiles faire Britomart, whose constant mind
Would not so lightly follow beauties chace,
Ne reckt of ladies love, did stay behynd,
And them awayted there a certaine space,
To weet if they would turne backe to that place:
But when she saw them gone, she forward went,
As lay her journey, through that perlous pace,
With stedfast corage and stout hardiment;
Ne evil thing she feard, ne evill thing she ment.

XX
At last, as nigh out of the wood she came,
A stately castle far away she spyde,
To which her steps directly she did frame.
That castle was most goodly edifyde,
And plaste for pleasure nigh that forrest syde:
But faire before the gate a spatious playne,
Mantled with greene, it selfe did spredden wyde,
On which she saw six knights, that did darrayne
Fiers battaill against one, with cruel might and mayne.

XXI
Mainely they all attonce upon him laid,
And sore beset on every side arownd,
That nigh he breathlesse grew, yet nought dismaid,
Ne ever to them yielded foot of grownd,
All had he lost much blood through many a wownd,
But stoutly dealt his blowes, and every way,
To which he turned in his wrathfull stownd,
Made them recoile, and fly from dredd decay,
That none of all the six before him durst assay.

XXII
Like dastard curres, that, having at a bay
The salvage beast embost in wearie chace,

Dare not adventure on the stubborne pray,
Ne byte before, but rome from place to place,
To get a snatch, when turned is his face.
In such distresse and doubtfull jeopardy
When Britomart him saw, she ran apace
Unto his reskew, and with earnest cry
Badd those same sixe forbeare that single enimy.

XXIII
But to her cry they list not lenden eare,
Ne ought the more their mightie strokes surceasse,
But gathering him rownd about more neare,
Their direfull rancour rather did encreasse;
Till that she, rushing through the thickest preasse,
Perforce disparted their compacted gyre,
And soone compeld to hearken unto peace:
Tho gan she myldly of them to inquyre
The cause of their dissention and outrageous yre.

XXIV
Whereto that single knight did answere frame:
'These six would me enforce by oddes of might,
To chaunge my liefe, and love another dame,
That death me liefer were then such despight,
So unto wrong to yield my wrested right:
For I love one, the truest one on grownd,
Ne list me chaunge; she th' Errant Damzell hight;
For whose deare sake full many a bitter stownd
I have endurd, and tasted many a bloody wownd.'

XXV
'Certes,' said she, 'then beene ye sixe to blame,
To weene your wrong by force to justify:
For knight to leave his lady were great shame,
That faithfull is, and better were to dy.
All losse is lesse, and lesse the infamy,
Then losse of love to him that loves but one:
Ne may love be compeld by maistery;
For soone as maistery comes, sweet Love anone
Taketh his nimble winges, and soone away is gone.'

XXVI
Then spake one of those six: 'There dwelleth here,
Within this castle wall, a lady fayre,
Whose soveraine beautie hath no living pere;
Thereto so bounteous and so debonayre,
That never any mote with her compayre.
She hath ordaind this law, which we approve,
That every knight, which doth this way repayre,
In case he have no lady nor no love,
Shall doe unto her service, never to remove.

XXVII
'But if he have a lady or a love,
Then must he her forgoe with fowle defame,
Or els with us by dint of sword approve,
That she is fairer then our fairest dame;
As did this knight, before ye hether came.'
'Perdy,' said Britomart, 'the choise is hard:
But what reward had he that overcame?'
'He should advaunced bee to high regard,'
Said they, 'and have our ladies love for his reward.

XXVIII
'Therefore aread, sir, if thou have a love.'
'Love have I sure,' quoth she, 'but lady none;
Yet will I not fro mine owne love remove,
Ne to your lady will I service done,
But wreake your wronges wrought to this knight alone,
And prove his cause.' With that, her mortall speare
She mightily aventred towards one,
And downe him smot ere well aware he weare;
Then to the next she rode, and downe the next did beare.

XXIX
Ne did she stay, till three on ground she layd,
That none of them himselfe could reare againe;
The fourth was by that other knight dismayd,
All were he wearie of his former paine,
That now there do but two of six remaine;
Which two did yield before she did them smight.
'Ah!' sayd she then, 'now may ye all see plaine,
That truth is strong, and trew love most of might,
That for his trusty servaunts doth so strongly fight.'

XXX
'Too well we see,' saide they, 'and prove too well
Our faulty weakenes, and your matchlesse might:
Forthy, faire sir, yours be the damozell,
Which by her owne law to your lot doth light,
And we your liege men faith unto you plight.'
So underneath her feet their swords they mard,
And after, her besought, well as they might,
To enter in and reape the dew reward:
She graunted, and then in they all together far'd.

XXXI
Long were it to describe the goodly frame
And stately port of Castle Joyeous,
(For so that castle hight by commun name)
Where they were entertaynd with courteous
And comely glee of many gratious

Faire ladies, and of many a gentle knight,
Who through a chamber long and spacious,
Eftsoones them brought unto their ladies sight,
That of them cleeped was the Lady of Delight.

XXXII
But for to tell the sumptuous aray
Of that great chamber should be labour lost:
For living wit, I weene, cannot display
The roiall riches and exceeding cost
Of every pillous and of every post;
Which all of purest bullion framed were,
And with great perles and pretious stones embost,
That the bright glister of their beames cleare
Did sparckle forth great light, and glorious did appeare.

XXXIII
These stranger knights, through passing, forth were led
Into an inner rowme, whose royaltee
And rich purveyance might uneath be red;
Mote princes place beseeme so deckt to bee.
Which stately manner when as they did see,
The image of superfluous riotize,
Exceeding much the state of meane degree,
They greatly wondred whence so sumpteous guize
Might be maintaynd, and each gan diversely devize.

XXXIV
The wals were round about appareiled
With costly clothes of Arras and of Toure,
In which with cunning hand was pourtrahed
The love of Venus and her paramoure,
The fayre Adonis, turned to a flowre,
A worke of rare device and wondrous wit.
First did it shew the bitter balefull stowre,
Which her assayd with many a fervent fit,
When first her tender hart was with his beautie smit:

XXXV
Then with what sleights and sweet allurements she
Entyst the boy, as well that art she knew,
And wooed him her paramoure to bee;
Now making girlonds of each flowre that grew,
To crowne his golden lockes with honour dew;
Now leading him into a secret shade
From his beauperes, and from bright heavens vew,
Where him to sleepe she gently would perswade,
Or bathe him in a fountaine by some covert glade.

XXXVI
And whilst he slept, she over him would spred

Her mantle, colour'd like the starry skyes,
And her soft arme lay underneath his hed,
And with ambrosiall kisses bathe his eyes;
And whilst he bath'd, with her two crafty spyes
She secretly would search each daintie lim,
And throw into the well sweet rosemaryes,
And fragrant violets, and paunces trim,
And ever with sweet nectar she did sprinkle him.

XXXVII
So did she steale his heedelesse hart away,
And joyd his love in secret unespyde.
But for she saw him bent to cruell play,
To hunt the salvage beast in forrest wyde,
Dreadfull of daunger, that mote him betyde,
She oft and oft adviz'd him to refraine
From chase of greater beastes, whose brutish pryde
Mote breede him scath unwares: but all in vaine;
For who can shun the chance that dest'ny doth ordaine?

XXXVIII
Lo! where beyond he lyeth languishing,
Deadly engored of a great wilde bore,
And by his side the goddesse groveling
Makes for him endlesse mone, and evermore
With her soft garment wipes away the gore,
Which staynes his snowy skin with hatefull hew:
But when she saw no helpe might him restore,
Him to a dainty flowre she did transmew,
Which in that cloth was wrought, as if it lively grew.

XXXIX
So was that chamber clad in goodly wize:
And rownd about it many beds were dight,
As whylome was the antique worldes guize,
Some for untimely ease, some for delight,
As pleased them to use, that use it might:
And all was full of damzels and of squyres,
Dauncing and reveling both day and night,
And swimming deepe in sensuall desyres;
And Cupid still emongest them kindled lustfull fyres.

XL
And all the while sweet musicke did divide
Her looser notes with Lydian harmony;
And all the while sweet birdes thereto applide
Their daintie layes and dulcet melody,
Ay caroling of love and jollity,
That wonder was to heare their trim consort.
Which when those knights beheld, with scornefull eye,
They sdeigned such lascivious disport,

And loath'd the loose demeanure of that wanton sort.

XLI
Thence they were brought to that great ladies vew,
Whom they found sitting on a sumptuous bed,
That glistred all with gold and glorious shew,
As the proud Persian queenes accustomed:
She seemed a woman of great bountihed
And of rare beautie, saving that askaunce
Her wanton eyes, ill signes of womanhed,
Did roll too lightly, and too often glaunce,
Without regard of grace or comely amenaunce.

XLII
Long worke it were, and needlesse, to devize
Their goodly entertainement and great glee:
She caused them be led in courteous wize
Into a bowre, disarmed for to be,
And cheared well with wine and spiceree:
The Redcrosse Knight was soone disarmed there,
But the brave mayd would not disarmed bee,
But onely vented up her umbriere.
And so did let her goodly visage to appere.

XLIII
As when fayre Cynthia, in darkesome night,
Is in a noyous cloud enveloped,
Where she may finde the substance thin and light
Breakes forth her silver beames, and her bright hed
Discovers to the world discomfited;
Of the poore traveiler, that went astray,
With thousand blessings she is heried;
Such was the beautie and the shining ray,
With which fayre Britomart gave light unto the day.

XLIV
And eke those six, which lately with her fought,
Now were disarmd, and did them selves present
Unto her vew, and company unsought;
For they all seemed courteous and gent,
And all sixe brethren, borne of one parent,
Which had them traynd in all civilitee,
And goodly taught to tilt and turnament;
Now were they liegmen to this ladie free,
And her knights service ought, to hold of her in fee.

XLV
The first of them by name Gardante hight,
A jolly person, and of comely vew;
The second was Parlante, a bold knight,
And next to him Jocante did ensew;

Basciante did him selfe most courteous shew;
But fierce Bacchante seemd too fell and keene;
And yett in armes Noctante greater grew:
All were faire knights, and goodly well beseene,
But to faire Britomart they all but shadowes beene.

XLVI
For shee was full of amiable grace,
And manly terror mixed therewithall,
That as the one stird up affections bace,
So th' other did mens rash desires apall,
And hold them backe, that would in error fall;
As hee that hath espide a vermeill rose,
To which sharpe thornes and breres the way forstall,
Dare not for dread his hardy hand expose,
But wishing it far off, his ydle wish doth lose.

XLVII
Whom when the lady saw so faire a wight,
All ignorant of her contrary sex,
(For shee her weend a fresh and lusty knight)
Shee greatly gan enamoured to wex,
And with vaine thoughts her falsed fancy vex:
Her fickle hart conceived hasty fyre,
Like sparkes of fire which fall in sclender flex,
That shortly brent into extreme desyre,
And ransackt all her veines with passion entyre.

XLVIII
Eftsoones shee grew to great impatience,
And into termes of open outrage brust,
That plaine discovered her incontinence,
Ne reckt shee who her meaning did mistrust;
For she was given all to fleshly lust,
And poured forth in sensuall delight,
That all regard of shame she had discust,
And meet respect of honor putt to flight:
So shamelesse beauty soone becomes a loathly sight.

XLIX
Faire ladies, that to love captived arre,
And chaste desires doe nourish in your mind,
Let not her fault your sweete affections marre,
Ne blott the bounty of all womankind,
'Mongst thousands good one wanton dame to find:
Emongst the roses grow some wicked weeds:
For this was not to love, but lust, inclind;
For love does alwaies bring forth bounteous deeds,
And in each gentle hart desire of honor breeds.

L

Nought so of love this looser dame did skill,
But as a cole to kindle fleshly flame,
Giving the bridle to her wanton will,
And treading under foote her honest name:
Such love is hate, and such desire is shame.
Still did she rove at her with crafty glaunce
Of her false eies, that at her hart did ayme,
And told her meaning in her countenaunce;
But Britomart dissembled it with ignoraunce.

LI
Supper was shortly dight, and downe they satt;
Where they were served with all sumptuous fare,
Whiles fruitfull Ceres and Lyæus fatt
Pourd out their plenty, without spight or spare:
Nought wanted there that dainty was and rare;
And aye the cups their bancks did overflow,
And aye, betweene the cups, she did prepare
Way to her love, and secret darts did throw;
But Britomart would not such guilfull message know.

LII
So when they slaked had the fervent heat
Of appetite with meates of every sort,
The lady did faire Britomart entreat,
Her to disarme, and with delightfull sport
To loose her warlike limbs and strong effort:
But when shee mote not thereunto be wonne,
(For shee her sexe under that straunge purport
Did use to hide, and plaine apparaunce shonne,)
In playner wise to tell her grievaunce she begonne.

LIII
And all attonce discovered her desire
With sighes, and sobs, and plaints, and piteous griefe,
The outward sparkes of her inburning fire;
Which spent in vaine, at last she told her briefe,
That, but if she did lend her short reliefe,
And doe her comfort, she mote algates dye.
But the chaste damzell, that had never priefe
Of such malengine and fine forgerye,
Did easely beleeve her strong extremitye.

LIV
Full easy was for her to have beliefe,
Who by self-feeling of her feeble sexe,
And by long triall of the inward griefe,
Wherewith imperious love her hart did vexe,
Could judge what paines doe loving harts perplexe.
Who meanes no guile, be guiled soonest shall,
And to faire semblaunce doth light faith annexe:

The bird, that knowes not the false fowlers call,
Into his hidden nett full easely doth fall.

LV
Forthy she would not in discourteise wise
Scorne the faire offer of good will profest;
For great rebuke it is, love to despise,
Or rudely sdeigne a gentle harts request;
But with faire countenaunce, as beseemed best,
Her entertaynd; nath'lesse shee inly deemd
Her love too light, to wooe a wandring guest:
Which she misconstruing, thereby esteemd
That from like inward fire that outward smoke had steemd.

LVI
Therewith a while she her flit fancy fedd,
Till she mote winne fit time for her desire,
But yet her wound still inward freshly bledd,
And through her bones the false instilled fire
Did spred it selfe, and venime close inspire.
Tho were the tables taken all away,
And every knight, and every gentle squire
Gan choose his dame with basciomani gay,
With whom he ment to make his sport and courtly play.

LVII
Some fell to daunce, some fel to hazardry,
Some to make love, some to make meryment,
As diverse witts to diverse things apply;
And all the while faire Malecasta bent
Her crafty engins to her close intent.
By this th' eternall lampes, wherewith high Jove
Doth light the lower world, were halfe yspent,
And the moist daughters of huge Atlas strove
Into the ocean deepe to drive their weary drove.

LVIII
High time it seemed then for everie wight
Them to betake unto their kindly rest:
Eftesoones long waxen torches weren light,
Unto their bowres to guyden every guest:
Tho, when the Britonesse saw all the rest
Avoided quite, she gan her selfe despoile,
And safe committ to her soft fethered nest,
Wher through long watch, and late daies weary toile,
She soundly slept, and carefull thoughts did quite assoile.

LIX
Now whenas all the world in silence deepe
Yshrowded was, and every mortall wight
Was drowned in the depth of deadly sleepe,

Faire Malecasta, whose engrieved spright
Could find no rest in such perplexed plight,
Lightly arose out of her wearie bed,
And, under the blacke vele of guilty night,
Her with a scarlott mantle covered,
That was with gold and ermines faire enveloped.

LX
Then panting softe, and trembling every joynt,
Her fearfull feete towards the bowre she mov'd,
Where she for secret purpose did appoynt
To lodge the warlike maide, unwisely loov'd;
And to her bed approching, first she proov'd
Whether she slept or wakte; with her softe hand
She softely felt if any member moov'd,
And lent her wary eare to understand
If any puffe of breath or signe of sence shee fond.

LXI
Which whenas none she fond, with easy shifte,
For feare least her unwares she should abrayd,
Th' embroderd quilt she lightly up did lifte,
And by her side her selfe she softly layd,
Of every finest fingers touch affrayd;
Ne any noise she made, ne word she spake,
But inly sigh'd. At last the royall mayd
Out of her quiet slomber did awake,
And chaungd her weary side, the better ease to take.

LXII
Where feeling one close couched by her side,
She lightly lept out of her filed bedd,
And to her weapon ran, in minde to gride
The loathed leachour. But the dame, halfe dedd
Through suddein feare and ghastly drerihedd,
Did shrieke alowd, that through the hous it rong,
And the whole family, therewith adredd,
Rashly out of their rouzed couches sprong,
And to the troubled chamber all in armes did throng.

LXIII
And those six knights, that ladies champions,
And eke the Redcrosse Knight ran to the stownd,
Halfe armd and halfe unarmd, with them attons:
Where when confusedly they came, they fownd
Their lady lying on the sencelesse grownd;
On thother side, they saw the warlike mayd
Al in her snow-white smocke, with locks unbownd,
Threatning the point of her avenging blaed;
That with so troublous terror they were all dismayd.

LXIV
About their ladye first they flockt arownd;
Whom having laid in comfortable couch,
Shortly they reard out of her frosen swownd;
And afterwardes they gan with fowle reproch
To stirre up strife, and troublous contecke broch:
But, by ensample of the last dayes losse,
None of them rashly durst to her approch,
Ne in so glorious spoile themselves embosse:
Her succourd eke the champion of the bloody crosse.

LXV
But one of those six knights, Gardante hight,
Drew out a deadly bow and arrow keene,
Which forth he sent with felonous despight,
And fell intent, against the virgin sheene:
The mortall steele stayd not till it was seene
To gore her side; yet was the wound not deepe,
But lightly rased her soft silken skin,
That drops of purple blood thereout did weepe,
Which did her lilly smock with staines of vermeil steep.

LXVI
Wherewith enrag'd, she fiercely at them flew,
And with her flaming sword about her layd,
That none of them foule mischiefe could eschew,
But with her dreadful strokes were all dismayd:
Here, there, and every where about her swayd
Her wrathfull steele, that none mote it abyde;
And eke the Redcrosse Knight gave her good ayd,
Ay joyning foot to foot, and syde to syde,
That in short space their foes they have quite terrifyde.

LXVII
Tho whenas all were put to shamefull flight,
The noble Britomartis her arayd,
And her bright armes about her body dight:
For nothing would she lenger there be stayd,
Where so loose life, and so ungentle trade,
Was usd of knights and ladies seeming gent:
So, earely, ere the grosse earthes gryesy shade
Was all disperst out of the firmament,
They tooke their steeds, and forth upon their journey went.

CANTO II

The Redcrosse Knight to Britomart
Describeth Artegall:

The wondrous myrrhour, by which she
In love with him did fall.

I
Here have I cause in men just blame to find,
That in their proper praise too partiall bee,
And not indifferent to woman kind,
To whom no share in armes and chevalree
They doe impart, ne maken memoree
Of their brave gestes and prowesse martiall:
Scarse doe they spare to one, or two, or three,
Rowme in their writtes; yet the same writing small
Does all their deedes deface, and dims their glories all.

II
But by record of antique times I finde,
That wemen wont in warres to beare most sway,
And to all great exploites them selves inclind:
Of which they still the girlond bore away,
Till envious men, fearing their rules decay,
Gan coyne streight lawes to curb their liberty:
Yet sith they warlike armes have laide away,
They have exceld in artes and pollicy,
That now we foolish men that prayse gin eke t' envy.

III
Of warlike puissaunce in ages spent,
Be thou, faire Britomart, whose prayse I wryte;
But of all wisedom bee thou precedent,
O soveraine Queene, whose prayse I would endyte,
Endite I would as dewtie doth excyte;
But ah! my rymes to rude and rugged arre,
When in so high an object they doe lyte,
And, striving fit to make, I feare doe marre:
Thy selfe thy prayses tell, and make them knowen farre.

IV
She, traveiling with Guyon, by the way
Of sondry thinges faire purpose gan to find,
T' abridg their journey long and lingring day:
Mongst which it fell into that Fairies mind
To aske this Briton maid, what uncouth wind
Brought her into those partes, and what inquest
Made her dissemble her disguised kind:
Faire lady she him seemd, like lady drest,
But fairest knight alive, when armed was her brest.

V
Thereat she sighing softly, had no powre
To speake a while, ne ready answere make,

But with hart-thrilling throbs and bitter stowre,
As if she had a fever fitt, did quake,
And every daintie limbe with horrour shake,
And ever and anone the rosy red
Flasht through her face, as it had beene a flake
Of lightning through bright heven fulmined:
At last, the passion past, she thus him answered:

VI
'Faire sir, I let you weete, that from the howre
I taken was from nourses tender pap,
I have beene trained up in warlike stowre,
To tossen speare and shield, and to affrap
The warlike ryder to his most mishap:
Sithence I loathed have my life to lead,
As ladies wont, in pleasures wanton lap,
To finger the fine needle and nyce thread;
Me lever were with point of foemans speare be dead.

VII
'All my delight on deedes of armes is sett,
To hunt out perilles and adventures hard,
By sea, by land, where so they may be mett,
Onely for honour and for high regard,
Without respect of richesse or reward.
For such intent into these partes I came,
Withouten compasse or withouten card,
Far fro my native soyle, that is by name
The Greater Brytayne, here to seeke for praise and fame.

VIII
'Fame blazed hath, that here in Faery Lond
Doe many famous knightes and ladies wonne,
And many straunge adventures to bee fond,
Of which great worth and worship may be wonne,
Which I to prove, this voyage have begonne.
But mote I weet of you, right courteous knight,
Tydings of one, that hath unto me donne
Late foule dishonour and reprochfull spight,
The which I seeke to wreake, and Arthegall he hight.'

IX
The word gone out she backe againe would call,
As her repenting so to have missayd,
But that he it uptaking ere the fall,
Her shortly answered: 'Faire martiall mayd,
Certes ye misavised beene, t' upbrayd
A gentle knight with so unknightly blame:
For weet ye well, of all that ever playd
At tilt or tourney, or like warlike game,
The noble Arthegall hath ever borne the name.

X
'Forthy great wonder were it, if such shame
Should ever enter in his bounteous thought,
Or ever doe that mote deserven blame:
The noble corage never weeneth ought,
That may unworthy of it selfe be thought.
Therefore, faire damzell, be ye well aware,
Least that too farre ye have your sorrow sought:
You and your countrey both I wish welfare,
And honour both; for each of other worthy are.'

XI
The royall maid woxe inly wondrous glad,
To heare her love so highly magnifyde,
And joyd that ever she affixed had
Her hart on knight so goodly glorifyde,
How ever finely she it faind to hyde:
The loving mother, that nine monethes did beare,
In the deare closett of her painefull syde,
Her tender babe, it seeing safe appeare,
Doth not so much rejoyce as she rejoyced theare.

XII
But to occasion him to further talke,
To feed her humor with his pleasing style,
Her list in stryfull termes with him to balke,
And thus replyde: 'How ever, sir, ye fyle
Your courteous tongue, his prayses to compyle,
It ill beseemes a knight of gentle sort,
Such as ye have him boasted, to beguyle
A simple maide, and worke so hainous tort,
In shame of knighthood, as I largely can report.

XIII
'Let bee therefore my vengeaunce to disswade,
And read, where I that faytour false may find.'
'Ah! but if reason faire might you perswade
To slake your wrath, and mollify your mind,'
Said he, 'perhaps ye should it better find:
For hardie thing it is, to weene by might
That man to hard conditions to bind,
Or ever hope to match in equall fight,
Whose prowesse paragone saw never living wight.

XIV
'Ne soothlich is it easie for to read
Where now on earth, or how, he may be fownd;
For he ne wonneth in one certeine stead,
But restlesse walketh all the world arownd,
Ay doing thinges that to his fame redownd,

Defending ladies cause and orphans right,
Where so he heares that any doth confownd
Them comfortlesse, through tyranny or might:
So is his soveraine honour raisde to hevens hight.'

XV
His feeling wordes her feeble sence much pleased,
And softly sunck into her molten hart:
Hart that is inly hurt is greatly eased
With hope of thing that may allegge his smart;
For pleasing wordes are like to magick art,
That doth the charmed snake in slomber lay:
Such secrete ease felt gentle Britomart,
Yet list the same efforce with faind gainesay:
So dischord ofte in musick makes the sweeter lay:

XVI
And sayd: 'Sir knight, these ydle termes forbeare,
And sith it is uneath to finde his haunt,
Tell me some markes by which he may appeare,
If chaunce I him encounter paravaunt;
For perdy one shall other slay, or daunt:
What shape, what shield, what armes, what steed, what stedd,
And what so else his person most may vaunt.'
All which the Redcrosse Knight to point aredd,
And him in everie part before her fashioned.

XVII
Yet him in everie part before she knew,
How ever list her now her knowledge fayne,
Sith him whylome in Brytayne she did vew,
To her revealed in a mirrhour playne,
Whereof did grow her first engraffed payne,
Whose root and stalke so bitter yet did taste,
That, but the fruit more sweetnes did contayne,
Her wretched dayes in dolour she mote waste,
And yield the pray of love to lothsome death at last.

XVIII
By straunge occasion she did him behold,
And much more straungely gan to love his sight,
As it in bookes hath written beene of old.
In Deheubarth, that now South-Wales is hight,
What time King Ryence raign'd and dealed right,
The great magitien Merlin had deviz'd,
By his deepe science and hell-dreaded might,
A looking glasse, right wondrously aguiz'd,
Whose vertues through the wyde worlde soone were solemniz'd.

XIX
It vertue had to shew in perfect sight

What ever thing was in the world contaynd,
Betwixt the lowest earth and hevens hight,
So that it to the looker appertaynd;
What ever foe had wrought, or frend had faynd,
Therein discovered was, ne ought mote pas,
Ne ought in secret from the same remaynd;
Forthy it round and hollow shaped was,
Like to the world it selfe, and seemd a world of glas.

XX
Who wonders not, that reades so wonderous worke?
But who does wonder, that has red the towre,
Wherein th' Aegyptian Phao long did lurke
From all mens vew, that none might her discoure,
Yet she might all men vew out of her bowre?
Great Ptolomæe it for his lemans sake
Ybuilded all of glasse, by magicke powre,
And also it impregnable did make;
Yet when his love was false, he with a peaze it brake.

XXI
Such was the glassy globe, that Merlin made,
And gave unto King Ryence for his gard,
That never foes his kingdome might invade,
But he it knew at home before he hard
Tydings thereof, and so them still debar'd.
It was a famous present for a prince,
And worthy worke of infinite reward,
That treasons could bewray, and foes convince:
Happy this realme, had it remayned ever since!

XXII
One day it fortuned fayre Britomart
Into her fathers closet to repayre;
For nothing he from her reserv'd apart,
Being his onely daughter and his hayre:
Where when she had espyde that mirrhour fayre,
Her selfe awhile therein she vewd in vaine;
Tho her avizing of the vertues rare
Which thereof spoken were, she gan againe
Her to bethinke of that mote to her selfe pertaine.

XXIII
But as it falleth, in the gentlest harts
Imperious Love hath highest set his throne,
And tyrannizeth in the bitter smarts
Of them that to him buxome are and prone:
So thought this mayd (as maydens use to done)
Whom fortune for her husband would allot;
Not that she lusted after any one,
For she was pure from blame of sinfull blot,

Yet wist her life at last must lincke in that same knot.

XXIV
Eftsoones there was presented to her eye
A comely knight, all arm'd in complete wize,
Through whose bright ventayle, lifted up on hye,
His manly face, that did his foes agrize,
And frends to termes of gentle truce entize,
Lookt foorth, as Phœbus face out of the east
Betwixt two shady mountaynes doth arize:
Portly his person was, and much increast
Through his heroicke grace and honorable gest.

XXV
His crest was covered with a couchant hownd,
And all his armour seemd of antique mould,
But wondrous massy and assured sownd,
And round about yfretted all with gold,
In which there written was, with cyphres old,
Achilles armes, which Arthegall did win.
And on his shield enveloped sevenfold
He bore a crowned litle ermilin,
That deckt the azure field with her fayre pouldred skin.

XXVI
The damzell well did vew his personage,
And liked well, ne further fastned not,
But went her way; ne her unguilty age
Did weene, unwares, that her unlucky lot
Lay hidden in the bottome of the pot:
Of hurt unwist most daunger doth redound:
But the false archer, which that arrow shot
So slyly that she did not feele the wound,
Did smyle full smoothly at her weetlesse wofull stound.

XXVII
Thenceforth the fether in her lofty crest,
Ruffed of love, gan lowly to availe,
And her prowd portaunce and her princely gest,
With which she earst tryumphed, now did quaile:
Sad, solemne, sowre, and full of fancies fraile
She woxe; yet wist she nether how, nor why;
She wist not, silly mayd, what she did aile,
Yet wist she was not well at ease perdy,
Yet thought it was not love, but some melancholy.

XXVIII
So soone as Night had with her pallid hew
Defaste the beautie of the shyning skye,
And reft from men the worldes desired vew,
She with her nourse adowne to sleepe did lye;

But sleepe full far away from her did fly:
In stead thereof sad sighes and sorrowes deepe
Kept watch and ward about her warily,
That nought she did but wayle, and often steepe
Her dainty couch with teares, which closely she did weepe.

XXIX
And if that any drop of slombring rest
Did chaunce to still into her weary spright,
When feeble nature felt her selfe opprest,
Streight way with dreames, and with fantastick sight
Of dreadfull things, the same was put to flight,
That oft out of her bed she did astart,
As one with vew of ghastly feends affright:
Tho gan she to renew her former smart,
And thinke of that fayre visage, written in her hart.

XXX
One night, when she was tost with such unrest,
Her aged nourse, whose name was Glauce hight,
Feeling her leape out of her loathed nest,
Betwixt her feeble armes her quickly keight,
And downe againe in her warme bed her dight:
'Ah! my deare daughter, ah! my dearest dread,
What uncouth fit,' sayd she, 'what evill plight,
Hath thee opprest, and with sad dreary-head
Chaunged thy lively cheare, and living made thee dead?

XXXI
'For not of nought these suddein ghastly feares
All night afflict thy naturall repose;
And all the day, when as thine equall peares
Their fit disports with faire delight doe chose,
Thou in dull corners doest thy selfe inclose,
Ne tastest princes pleasures, ne doest spred
Abroad thy fresh youths fayrest flowre, but lose
Both leafe and fruite, both too untimely shed,
As one in wilfull bale for ever buried.

XXXII
'The time that mortall men their weary cares
Do lay away, and all wilde beastes do rest,
And every river eke his course forbeares,
Then doth this wicked evill thee infest,
And rive with thousand throbs thy thrilled brest;
Like an huge Aetn' of deepe engulfed gryefe,
Sorrow is heaped in thy hollow chest,
Whence foorth it breakes in sighes and anguish ryfe,
As smoke and sulphure mingled with confused stryfe.

XXXIII

'Ay me! how much I feare least love it bee!
But if that love it be, as sure I read
By knowen signes and passions which I see,
Be it worthy of thy race and royall sead,
Then I avow by this most sacred head
Of my deare foster childe, to ease thy griefe,
And win thy will: therefore away doe dread;
For death nor daunger from thy dew reliefe
Shall me debarre: tell me, therefore, my liefest liefe.'

XXXIV
So having sayd, her twixt her armes twaine
Shee streightly straynd, and colled tenderly,
And every trembling joynt and every vaine
Shee softly felt, and rubbed busily,
To doe the frosen cold away to fly;
And her faire deawy eies with kisses deare
Shee ofte did bathe, and ofte againe did dry;
And ever her importund, not to feare
To let the secret of her hart to her appeare.

XXXV
The damzell pauzd, and then thus fearfully:
'Ah! nurse, what needeth thee to eke my paine?
Is not enough that I alone doe dye,
But it must doubled bee with death of twaine?
For nought for me but death there doth remaine.'
'O daughter deare,' said she, 'despeire no whit;
For never sore, but might a salve obtaine:
That blinded god, which hath ye blindly smit,
Another arrow hath your lovers hart to hit.'

XXXVI
'But mine is not,' quoth she, 'like other wownd;
For which no reason can finde remedy.'
'Was never such, but mote the like be fownd,'
Said she, 'and though no reason may apply
Salve to your sore, yet love can higher stye
Then reasons reach, and oft hath wonders donne.'
'But neither god of love nor god of skye
Can doe,' said she, 'that which cannot be donne.'
'Things ofte impossible,' quoth she, 'seeme ere begonne.'

XXXVII
'These idle wordes,' said she, 'doe nought aswage
My stubborne smart, but more annoiaunce breed:
For no no usuall fire, no usuall rage
Yt is, O nourse, which on my life doth feed,
And sucks the blood which from my hart doth bleed.
But since thy faithfull zele lets me not hyde
My crime, (if crime it be) I will it reed.

Nor prince, nor pere it is, whose love hath gryde
My feeble brest of late, and launched this wound wyde.

XXXVIII
'Nor man it is, nor other living wight;
For then some hope I might unto me draw;
But th' only shade and semblant of a knight,
Whose shape or person yet I never saw,
Hath me subjected to Loves cruell law:
The same one day, as me misfortune led,
I in my fathers wondrous mirrhour saw,
And, pleased with that seeming goodly-hed,
Unwares the hidden hooke with baite I swallowed.

XXXIX
'Sithens it hath infixed faster bold
Within my bleeding bowells, and so sore
Now ranckleth in this same fraile fleshly mould,
That all mine entrailes flow with poisnous gore,
And th' ulcer groweth daily more and more;
Ne can my ronning sore finde remedee,
Other then my hard fortune to deplore,
And languish as the leafe faln from the tree,
Till death make one end of my daies and miseree.'

XL
'Daughter,' said she, 'what need ye be dismayd,
Or why make ye such monster of your minde?
Of much more uncouth thing I was affrayd;
Of filthy lust, contrary unto kinde:
But this affection nothing straunge I finde;
For who with reason can you aye reprove,
To love the semblaunt pleasing most your minde,
And yield your heart whence ye cannot remove?
No guilt in you, but in the tyranny of Love.

XLI
'Not so th' Arabian Myrrhe did sett her mynd,
Nor so did Biblis spend her pining hart,
But lov'd their native flesh against al kynd,
And to their purpose used wicked art:
Yet playd Pasiphaë a more monstrous part,
That lov'd a bul, and learnd a beast to bee:
Such shamefull lusts who loaths not, which depart
From course of nature and of modestee?
Swete Love such lewdnes bands from his faire companee.

XLII
'But thine, my deare, (welfare thy heart, my deare)
Though straunge beginning had, yet fixed is
On one that worthy may perhaps appeare;

And certes seemes bestowed not amis:
Joy thereof have thou and eternall blis.'
With that upleaning on her elbow weake,
Her alablaster brest she soft did kis,
Which all that while shee felt to pant and quake,
As it an earth-quake were: at last she thus bespake:

XLIII
'Beldame, your words doe worke me litle ease;
For though my love be not so lewdly bent
As those ye blame, yet may it nought appease
My raging smart, ne ought my flame relent,
But rather doth my helpelesse griefe augment.
For they, how ever shamefull and unkinde,
Yet did possesse their horrible intent:
Short end of sorowes they therby did finde;
So was their fortune good, though wicked were their minde.

XLIV
'But wicked fortune mine, though minde be good,
Can have no end, nor hope of my desire,
But feed on shadowes, whiles I die for food,
And like a shadow wexe, whiles with entire
Affection I doe languish and expire.
I, fonder then Cephisus foolish chyld,
Who, having vewed in a fountaine shere
His face, was with the love thereof beguyld;
I, fonder, love a shade, the body far exyld.'

XLV
'Nought like,' quoth shee, 'for that same wretched boy
Was of him selfe the ydle paramoure,
Both love and lover, without hope of joy;
For which he faded to a watry flowre.
But better fortune thine, and better howre,
Which lov'st the shadow of a warlike knight;
No shadow, but a body hath in powre:
That body, wheresoever that it light,
May learned be by cyphers, or by magicke might.

XLVI
'But if thou may with reason yet represse
The growing evill, ere it strength have gott,
And thee abandoned wholy doe possesse,
Against it strongly strive, and yield thee nott,
Til thou in open fielde adowne be smott.
But if the passion mayster thy fraile might,
So that needs love or death must bee thy lott,
Then I avow to thee, by wrong or right
To compas thy desire, and find that loved knight.'

XLVII
Her chearefull words much cheard the feeble spright
Of the sicke virgin, that her downe she layd
In her warme bed to sleepe, if that she might;
And the old-woman carefully displayd
The clothes about her round with busy ayd,
So that at last a litle creeping sleepe
Surprisd her sence. Shee, therewith well apayd,
The dronken lamp down in the oyl did steepe,
And sett her by to watch, and sett her by to weepe.

XLVIII
Earely the morrow next, before that day
His joyous face did to the world revele,
They both uprose and tooke their ready way
Unto the church, their praiers to appele,
With great devotion, and with litle zele:
For the faire damzell from the holy herse
Her love-sicke hart to other thoughts did steale;
And that old dame said many an idle verse,
Out of her daughters hart fond fancies to reverse.

XLIX
Retourned home, the royall infant fell
Into her former fitt; forwhy no powre
Nor guidaunce of her selfe in her did dwell.
But th' aged nourse, her calling to her bowre,
Had gathered rew, and savine, and the flowre
Of camphora, and calamint, and dill,
All which she in a earthen pot did poure,
And to the brim with colt wood did it fill,
And many drops of milk and blood through it did spill.

L
Then, taking thrise three heares from of her head,
Them trebly breaded in a threefold lace,
And round about the pots mouth bound the thread,
And after having whispered a space
Certein sad words, with hollow voice and bace,
Shee to the virgin sayd, thrise sayd she itt:
'Come, daughter, come, come; spit upon my face,
Spitt thrise upon me, thrise upon me spitt;
Th' uneven number for this business is most fitt.'

LI
That sayd, her rownd about she from her turnd,
She turned her contrary to the sunne,
Thrise she her turnd contrary, and returnd
All contrary, for she the right did shunne,
And ever what she did was streight undonne.
So thought she to undoe her daughters love:

But love, that is in gentle brest begonne,
No ydle charmes so lightly may remove;
That well can witnesse, who by tryall it does prove.

LII
Ne ought it mote the noble mayd avayle,
Ne slake the fury of her cruell flame,
But that shee still did waste, and still did wayle,
That through long languour and hart-burning brame
She shortly like a pyned ghost became,
Which long hath waited by the Stygian strond.
That when old Glauce saw, for feare least blame
Of her miscarriage should in her be fond,
She wist not how t' amend, nor how it to withstond.

CANTO III

Merlin bewrayes to Britomart
The state of Arthegall:
And shews the famous progeny,
Which from them springen shall.

I
Most sacred fyre, that burnest mightily
In living brests, ykindled first above,
Emongst th' eternall spheres and lamping sky,
And thence pourd into men, which men call Love;
Not that same which doth base affections move
In brutish mindes, and filthy lust inflame,
But that sweete fit that doth true beautie love,
And choseth Vertue for his dearest dame,
Whence spring all noble deedes and never dying fame:

II
Well did antiquity a god thee deeme,
That over mortall mindes hast so great might,
To order them as best to thee doth seeme,
And all their actions to direct aright:
The fatall purpose of divine foresight
Thou doest effect in destined descents,
Through deepe impression of thy secret might,
And stirredst up th' heroes high intents,
Which the late world admyres for wondrous moniments.

III
But thy dredd dartes in none doe triumph more,
Ne braver proofe, in any, of thy powre

Shew'dst thou, then in this royall maid of yore,
Making her seeke an unknowne paramoure,
From the worlds end, through many a bitter stowre:
From whose two loynes thou afterwardes did rayse
Most famous fruites of matrimoniall bowre,
Which through the earth have spredd their living prayse,
That Fame in tromp of gold eternally displayes.

IV
Begin then, O my dearest sacred dame,
Daughter of Phœbus and of Memorye,
That doest ennoble with immortall name
The warlike worthies, from antiquitye,
In thy great volume of eternitye:
Begin, O Clio, and recount from hence
My glorious Soveraines goodly auncestrye,
Till that by dew degrees and long protense,
Thou have it lastly brought unto her Excellence.

V
Full many wayes within her troubled mind
Old Glauce east, to cure this ladies griefe:
Full many waies she sought, but none could find,
Nor herbes, nor charmes, nor counsel, that is chiefe
And choisest med'cine for sick harts reliefe:
Forthy great care she tooke, and greater feare,
Least that it should her turne to fowle repriefe
And sore reproch, when so her father deare
Should of his dearest daughters hard misfortune heare.

VI
At last she her avisde, that he which made
That mirrhour, wherein the sicke damosell
So straungely vewed her straunge lovers shade,
To weet, the learned Merlin, well could tell,
Under what coast of heaven the man did dwell,
And by what means his love might best be wrought:
For though beyond the Africk Ismael
Or th' Indian Peru he were, she thought
Him forth through infinite endevour to have sought.

VII
Forthwith them selves disguising both in straunge
And base atyre, that none might them bewray,
To Maridunum, that is now by chaunge
Of name Cayr-Merdin cald, they tooke their way:
There the wise Merlin whylome wont (they say)
To make his wonne, low underneath the ground,
In a deepe delve, farre from the vew of day,
That of no living wight he mote be found,
When so he counseld with his sprights encompast round.

VIII
And if thou ever happen that same way
To traveill, go to see that dreadfull place:
It is an hideous hollow cave (they say)
Under a rock, that lyes a litle space
From the swift Barry, tombling downe apace
Emongst the woody hilles of Dynevowre:
But dare thou not, I charge, in any cace,
To enter into that same balefull bowre,
For feare the cruell feendes should thee unwares devowre.

IX
But standing high aloft, low lay thine eare,
And there such ghastly noyse of yron chaines
And brasen caudrons thou shalt rombling heare,
Which thousand sprights with long enduring paines
Doe tosse, that it will stonn thy feeble braines;
And oftentimes great grones, and grievous stownds,
When too huge toile and labour them constraines,
And oftentimes loud strokes, and ringing sowndes,
From under that deepe rock most horribly rebowndes.

X
The cause, some say, is this: A litle whyle
Before that Merlin dyde, he did intend
A brasen wall in compas to compyle
About Cairmardin, and did it commend
Unto these sprights, to bring to perfect end.
During which worke the Lady of the Lake,
Whom long he lov'd, for him in hast did send;
Who, thereby forst his workemen to forsake,
Them bownd, till his retourne, their labour not to slake.

XI
In the meane time, through that false ladies traine,
He was surprisd, and buried under beare,
Ne ever to his worke returnd againe:
Nath'lesse those feends may not their work forbeare,
So greatly his commandement they feare,
But there doe toyle and traveile day and night,
Untill that brasen wall they up doe reare:
For Merlin had in magick more insight
Then ever him before or after living wight.

XII
For he by wordes could call out of the sky
Both sunne and moone, and make them him obay:
The land to sea, and sea to maineland dry,
And darksom night he eke could turne to day:
Huge hostes of men he could alone dismay,

And hostes of men of meanest thinges could frame,
When so him list his enimies to fray:
That to this day, for terror of his fame,
The feends do quake, when any him to them does name.

XIII
And sooth, men say that he was not the sonne
Of mortall syre or other living wight,
But wondrously begotten, and begonne
By false illusion of a guilefull spright
On a faire lady nonne, that whilome hight
Matilda, daughter to Pubidius,
Who was the lord of Mathraval by right,
And coosen unto King Ambrosius:
Whence he indued was with skill so merveilous.

XIV
They, here ariving, staid a while without,
Ne durst adventure rashly in to wend,
But of their first intent gan make new dout,
For dread of daunger, which it might portend:
Untill the hardy mayd (with love to frend)
First entering, the dreadfull mage there fownd
Deepe busied bout worke of wondrous end,
And writing straunge characters in the grownd,
With which the stubborne feendes he to his service bownd.

XV
He nought was moved at their entraunce bold,
For of their comming well he wist afore;
Yet list them bid their businesse to unfold,
As if ought in this world in secrete store
Were from him hidden, or unknowne of yore.
Then Glauce thus: 'Let not it thee offend,
That we thus rashly through thy darksom dore
Unwares have prest: for either fatall end,
Or other mightie cause, us two did hether send.'

XVI
He bad tell on; and then she thus began:
'Now have three moones with borrowd brothers light
Thrise shined faire, and thrise seemd dim and wan,
Sith a sore evill, which this virgin bright
Tormenteth, and doth plonge in dolefull plight,
First rooting tooke; but what thing it mote bee,
Or whence it sprong, I can not read aright;
But this I read, that, but if remedee
Thou her afford, full shortly I her dead shall see.'

XVII
Therewith th' enchaunter softly gan to smyle

At her smooth speeches, weeting inly well
That she to him dissembled womanish guyle,
And to her said: 'Beldame, by that ye tell,
More neede of leach-crafte hath your damozell,
Then of my skill: who helpe may have elswhere,
In vaine seekes wonders out of magick spell.'
Th' old woman wox half blanck those wordes to heare;
And yet was loth to let her purpose plaine appeare;

XVIII
And to him said: 'Yf any leaches skill,
Or other learned meanes, could have redrest
This my deare daughters deepe engraffed ill,
Certes I should be loth thee to molest:
But this sad evill, which doth her infest,
Doth course of naturall cause farre exceed,
And housed is within her hollow brest,
That either seemes some cursed witches deed,
Or evill spright, that in her doth such torment breed.'

XIX
The wisard could no lenger beare her bord,
But brusting forth in laughter, to her sayd:
'Glauce, what needes this colourable word,
To cloke the cause that hath it selfe bewrayd?
Ne ye, fayre Britomartis, thus arayd,
More hidden are then sunne in cloudy vele;
Whom thy good fortune, having fate obayd,
Hath hether brought, for succour to appele:
The which the Powres to thee are pleased to revele.'

XX
The doubtfull mayd, seeing her selfe descryde,
Was all abasht, and her pure yvory
Into a cleare carnation suddeine dyde;
As fayre Aurora, rysing hastily,
Doth by her blushing tell that she did lye
All night in old Tithonus frosen bed,
Whereof she seemes ashamed inwardly.
But her olde nourse was nought dishartened,
But vauntage made of that which Merlin had ared;

XXI
And sayd: 'Sith then thou knowest all our griefe,
(For what doest not thou knowe?) of grace, I pray,
Pitty our playnt, and yield us meet reliefe.'
With that the prophet still awhile did stay,
And then his spirite thus gan foorth display:
'Most noble virgin, that by fatall lore
Hast learn'd to love, let no whit thee dismay
The hard beginne that meetes thee in the dore,

And with sharpe fits thy tender hart oppresseth sore.

XXII
'For so must all things excellent begin,
And eke enrooted deepe must be that tree,
Whose big embodied braunches shall not lin,
Till they to hevens hight forth stretched bee.
For from thy wombe a famous progenee
Shall spring, out of the aunciant Trojan blood,
Which shall revive the sleeping memoree
Of those same antique peres, the hevens brood,
Which Greeke and Asian rivers stayned with their blood.

XXIII
'Renowmed kings and sacred emperours,
Thy fruitfull ofspring, shall from thee descend;
Brave captaines and most mighty warriours,
That shall their conquests through all lands extend,
And their decayed kingdomes shall amend:
The feeble Britons, broken with long warre,
They shall upreare, and mightily defend
Against their forren foe, that commes from farre,
Till universall peace compound all civill jarre.

XXIV
'It was not, Britomart, thy wandring eye,
Glauncing unwares in charmed looking glas,
But the streight course of hevenly destiny,
Led with Eternall Providence, that has
Guyded thy glaunce, to bring His will to pas:
Ne is thy fate, ne is thy fortune ill,
To love the prowest knight that ever was:
Therefore submit thy wayes unto His will,
And doe, by all dew meanes, thy destiny fulfill.'

XXV
'But read,' saide Glauce, 'thou magitian,
What meanes shall she out seeke, or what waies take?
How shall she know, how shall she finde the man?
Or what needes her to toyle, sith Fates can make
Way for themselves, their purpose to pertake?'
Then Merlin thus: 'Indeede the Fates are firme,
And may not shrinck, though all the world do shake:
Yet ought mens good endevours them confirme,
And guyde the heavenly causes to their constant terme.

XXVI
'The man, whom heavens have ordaynd to bee
The spouse of Britomart, is Arthegall:
He wonneth in the land of Fayeree,
Yet is no Fary borne, ne sib at all

To Elfes, but sprong of seed terrestriall,
And whylome by false Faries stolne away,
Whyles yet in infant cradle he did crall;
Ne other to himselfe is knowne this day,
But that he by an Elfe was gotten of a Fay.

XXVII
'But sooth he is the sonne of Gorlois,
And brother unto Cador, Cornish king,
And for his warlike feates renowmed is,
From where the day out of the sea doth spring
Untill the closure of the evening.
From thence him, firmely bound with faithfull band,
To this his native soyle thou backe shalt bring,
Strongly to ayde his countrey to withstand
The powre of forreine Paynims, which invade thy land.

XXVIII
'Great ayd thereto his mighty puissaunce
And dreaded name shall give in that sad day:
Where also proofe of thy prow valiaunce
Thou then shalt make, t' increase thy lovers pray.
Long time ye both in armes shall beare great sway,
Till thy wombes burden thee from them do call,
And his last fate him from thee take away,
Too rathe cut off by practise criminall
Of secrete foes, that him shall make in mischiefe fall.

XXIX
'With thee yet shall he leave, for memory
Of his late puissaunce, his ymage dead,
That living him in all activity
To thee shall represent. He from the head
Of his coosen Constantius, without dread,
Shall take the crowne, that was his fathers right,
And therewith crowne himselfe in th' others stead:
Then shall he issew forth with dreadfull might,
Against his Saxon foes in bloody field to fight.

XXX
'Like as a lyon, that in drowsie cave
Hath long time slept, himselfe so shall he shake,
And comming forth, shall spred his banner brave
Over the troubled South, that it shall make
The warlike Mertians for feare to quake:
Thrise shall he fight with them, and twise shall win,
But the third time shall fayre accordaunce make:
And if he then with victorie can lin,
He shall his dayes with peace bring to his earthly in.

XXXI

'His sonne, hight Vortipore, shall him succeede
In kingdome, but not in felicity;
Yet shall he long time warre with happy speed,
And with great honour many batteills try:
But at the last to th' importunity
Of froward fortune shall be forst to yield.
But his sonne Malgo shall full mightily
Avenge his fathers losse, with speare and shield,
And his proud foes discomfit in victorious field.

XXXII
'Behold the man! and tell me, Britomart,
If ay more goodly creature thou didst see:
How like a gyaunt in each manly part
Beares he himselfe with portly majestee,
That one of th' old heroes seemes to bee!
He the six islands, comprovinciall
In auncient times unto Great Britainee,
Shall to the same reduce, and to him call
Their sondry kings to doe their homage severall.

XXXIII
'All which his sonne Careticus awhile
Shall well defend, and Saxons powre suppresse,
Untill a straunger king, from unknowne soyle
Arriving, him with multitude oppresse;
Great Gormond, having with huge mightinesse
Ireland subdewd, and therein fixt his throne,
Like a swift otter, fell through emptinesse,
Shall overswim the sea with many one
Of his Norveyses, to assist the Britons fone.

XXXIV
'He in his furie all shall overronne,
And holy church with faithlesse handes deface,
That thy sad people, utterly fordonne,
Shall to the utmost mountaines fly apace:
Was never so great waste in any place,
Nor so fowle outrage doen by living men:
For all thy citties they shall sacke and race,
And the greene grasse that groweth they shall bren,
That even the wilde beast shall dy in starved den.

XXXV
'Whiles thus thy Britons doe in languour pine,
Proud Etheldred shall from the North arise,
Serving th' ambitious will of Augustine,
And passing Dee with hardy enterprise,
Shall backe repulse the valiaunt Brockwell twise,
And Bangor with massacred martyrs fill;
But the third time shall rew his foolhardise:

For Cadwan, pittying his peoples ill,
Shall stoutly him defeat, and thousand Saxons kill.

XXXVI
'But after him, Cadwallin mightily
On his sonne Edwin all those wrongs shall wreake;
Ne shall availe the wicked sorcery
Of false Pellite, his purposes to breake,
But him shall slay, and on a gallowes bleak
Shall give th' enchaunter his unhappy hire:
Then shall the Britons, late dismayd and weake,
From their long vassallage gin to respire,
And on their Paynim foes avenge their ranckled ire.

XXXVII
'Ne shall he yet his wrath so mitigate,
Till both the sonnes of Edwin he have slayne,
Offricke and Osricke, twinnes unfortunate,
Both slaine in battaile upon Layburne playne,
Together with the king of Louthiane,
Hight Adin, and the king of Orkeny,
Both joynt partakers of their fatall payne:
But Penda, fearefull of like desteny,
Shall yield him selfe his liegeman, and sweare fealty.

XXXVIII
'Him shall he make his fatall instrument,
T' afflict the other Saxons unsubdewd;
He marching forth with fury insolent
Against the good King Oswald, who, indewd
With heavenly powre, and by angels reskewd,
Al holding crosses in their hands on hye,
Shall him defeate withouten blood imbrewd:
Of which that field for endlesse memory
Shall Hevenfield be cald to all posteritie.

XXXIX
'Whereat Cadwallin wroth, shall forth issew,
And an huge hoste into Northumber lead,
With which he godly Oswald shall subdew,
And crowne with martiredome his sacred head.
Whose brother Oswin, daunted with like dread,
With price of silver shall his kingdome buy,
And Penda, seeking him adowne to tread,
Shall tread adowne, and doe him fowly dye,
But shall with guifts his lord Cadwallin pacify.

XL
'Then shall Cadwallin die, and then the raine
Of Britons eke with him attonce shall dye;
Ne shall the good Cadwallader, with paine

Or powre, be hable it to remedy,
When the full time, prefixt by destiny,
Shalbe expird of Britons regiment:
For Heven it selfe shall their successe envy,
And them with plagues and murrins pestilent
Consume, till all their warlike puissaunce be spent.

XLI
'Yet after all these sorrowes, and huge hills
Of dying people, during eight yeares space,
Cadwallader, not yielding to his ills,
From Armoricke, where long in wretched cace
He liv'd, retourning to his native place,
Shalbe by vision staide from his intent:
For th' Heavens have decreed to displace
The Britons for their sinnes dew punishment,
And to the Saxons over-give their government.

XLII
'Then woe, and woe, and everlasting woe,
Be to the Briton babe, that shalbe borne
To live in thraldome of his fathers foe!
Late king, now captive, late lord, now forlorne,
The worlds reproch, the cruell victors scorne,
Banisht from princely bowre to wasteful wood!
O! who shal helpe me to lament and mourne
The royall seed, the antique Trojan blood,
Whose empire lenger here then ever any stood?'

XLIII
The damzell was full deepe empassioned,
Both for his griefe, and for her peoples sake,
Whose future woes so plaine he fashioned,
And sighing sore, at length him thus bespake:
'Ah! but will Hevens fury never slake,
Nor vengeaunce huge relent it selfe at last?
Will not long misery late mercy make,
But shall their name for ever be defaste,
And quite from of the earth their memory be raste?'

XLIV
'Nay, but the terme,' sayd he, 'is limited,
That in this thraldome Britons shall abide,
And the just revolution measured,
That they as straungers shalbe notifide:
For twise fowre hundreth yeares shalbe supplide,
Ere they to former rule restor'd shalbee,
And their importune fates all satisfide:
Yet during this their most obscuritee,
Their beames shall ofte breake forth, that men them faire may see.

XLV
'For Rhodoricke, whose surname shalbe Great,
Shall of him selfe a brave ensample shew,
That Saxon kings his frendship shall intreat;
And Howell Dha shall goodly well indew
The salvage minds with skill of just and trew;
Then Griffyth Conan also shall up reare
His dreaded head, and the old sparkes renew
Of native corage, that his foes shall feare
Least back againe the kingdom he from them should beare.

XLVI
'Ne shall the Saxons selves all peaceably
Enjoy the crowne, which they from Britons wonne
First ill, and after ruled wickedly:
For ere two hundred yeares be full outronne,
There shall a Raven, far from rising sunne,
With his wide wings upon them fiercely fly,
And bid his faithlesse chickens overonne
The fruitfull plaines, and with fell cruelty,
In their avenge, tread downe the victors surquedry.

XLVII
'Yet shall a third both these and thine subdew:
There shall a Lion from the sea-bord wood
Of Neustria come roring, with a crew
Of hungry whelpes, his battailous bold brood,
Whose clawes were newly dipt in cruddy blood,
That from the Daniske tyrants head shall rend
Th' usurped crowne, as if that he were wood,
And the spoile of the countrey conquered
Emongst his young ones shall divide with bountyhed.

XLVIII
'Tho, when the terme is full accomplishid,
There shall a sparke of fire, which hath long-while
Bene in his ashes raked up and hid,
Bee freshly kindled in the fruitfull ile
Of Mona, where it lurked in exile;
Which shall breake forth into bright burning flame,
And reach into the house that beares the stile
Of roiall majesty and soveraine name:
So shall the Briton blood their crowne agayn reclame.

XLIX
'Thenceforth eternall union shall be made
Betweene the nations different afore,
And sacred Peace shall lovingly persuade
The warlike minds to learne her goodly lore,
And civile armes to exercise no more:
Then shall a royall Virgin raine, which shall

Stretch her white rod over the Belgicke shore,
And the great Castle smite so sore with all,
That it shall make him shake, and shortly learn to fall.

L
'But yet the end is not.——' There Merlin stayd,
As overcomen of the spirites powre,
Or other ghastly spectacle dismayd,
That secretly he saw, yet note discoure:
Which suddein fitt and halfe extatick stoure
When the two fearefull wemen saw, they grew
Greatly confused in behaveoure:
At last the fury past, to former hew
Hee turnd againe, and chearfull looks as earst did shew.

LI
Then, when them selves they well instructed had
Of all that needed them to be inquird,
They both, conceiving hope of comfort glad,
With lighter hearts unto their home retird;
Where they in secret counsell close conspird,
How to effect so hard an enterprize,
And to possesse the purpose they desird:
Now this, now that twixt them they did devize,
And diverse plots did frame, to maske in strange disguise.

LII
At last the nourse in her foolhardy wit
Conceivd a bold devise, and thus bespake:
'Daughter, I deeme that counsel aye most fit,
That of the time doth dew advauntage take:
Ye see that good King Uther now doth make
Strong warre upon the Paynim brethren, hight
Octa and Oza, whome hee lately brake
Beside Cayr Verolame in victorious fight,
That now all Britany doth burne in armes bright.

LIII
'That therefore nought our passage may empeach,
Let us in feigned armes our selves disguize,
And our weake hands (whom need new strength shall teach)
The dreadful speare and shield to exercize:
Ne certes, daughter, that same warlike wize,
I weene, would you misseeme; for ye beene tall
And large of limbe t' atchieve an hard emprize,
Ne ought ye want, but skil, which practize small
Wil bring, and shortly make you a mayd martiall.

LIV
'And sooth, it ought your corage much inflame,
To heare so often, in that royall hous,

From whence to none inferior ye came,
Bards tell of many wemen valorous,
Which have full many feats adventurous
Performd, in paragone of proudest men:
The bold Bunduca, whose victorious
Exployts made Rome to quake, stout Guendolen,
Renowmed Martia, and redoubted Emmilen;

LV
'And that which more then all the rest may sway,
Late dayes ensample, which these eyes beheld:
In the last field before Menevia,
Which Uther with those forrein pagans held,
I saw a Saxon virgin, the which feld
Great Ulfin thrise upon the bloody playne,
And had not Carados her hand withheld
From rash revenge, she had him surely slayne,
Yet Carados himselfe from her escapt with payne.'

LVI
'Ah! read,' quoth Britomart, 'how is she hight?'
'Fayre Angela,' quoth she, 'men do her call,
No whit lesse fayre then terrible in fight:
She hath the leading of a martiall
And mightie people, dreaded more then all
The other Saxons, which doe, for her sake
And love, themselves of her name Angles call.
Therefore, faire infant, her ensample make
Unto thy selfe, and equall corage to thee take.'

LVII
Her harty wordes so deepe into the mynd
Of the yong damzell sunke, that great desire
Of warlike armes in her forthwith they tynd,
And generous stout courage did inspyre,
That she resolv'd, unweeting to her syre,
Advent'rous knighthood on her selfe to don,
And counseld with her nourse, her maides attyre
To turne into a massy habergeon,
And bad her all things put in readinesse anon.

LVIII
Th' old woman nought that needed did omit;
But all thinges did conveniently purvay.
It fortuned (so time their turne did fitt)
A band of Britons, ryding on forray
Few dayes before, had gotten a great pray
Of Saxon goods, emongst the which was seene
A goodly armour, and full rich aray,
Which long'd to Angela, the Saxon queene,
All fretted round with gold, and goodly wel beseene.

LIX
The same, with all the other ornaments,
King Ryence caused to be hanged hy
In his chiefe church, for endlesse moniments
Of his successe and gladfull victory:
Of which her selfe avising readily,
In th' evening late old Glauce thether led
Faire Britomart, and that same armory
Downe taking, her therein appareled,
Well as she might, and with brave bauldrick garnished.

LX
Beside those armes there stood a mightie speare,
Which Bladud made by magick art of yore,
And usd the same in batteill aye to beare;
Sith which it had beene here preserv'd in store,
For his great vertues proved long afore:
For never wight so fast in sell could sit,
But him perforce unto the ground it bore:
Both speare she tooke and shield, which hong by it;
Both speare and shield of great powre, for her purpose fit.

LXI
Thus when she had the virgin all arayd,
Another harnesse, which did hang thereby,
About her selfe she dight, that the yong mayd
She might in equall armes accompany,
And as her squyre attend her carefully:
Tho to their ready steedes they clombe full light,
And through back waies, that none might them espy,
Covered with secret cloud of silent night,
Themselves they forth convaid, and passed forward right.

LXII
Ne rested they, till that to Faery Lond
They came, as Merlin them directed late:
Where meeting with this Redcrosse Knight, she fond
Of diverse thinges discourses to dilate,
But most of Arthegall and his estate.
At last their wayes so fell, that they mote part:
Then each to other well affectionate,
Frendship professed with unfained hart:
The Redcrosse Knight diverst, but forth rode Britomart.

CANTO IV

Bold Marinell of Britomart

Is throwne on the Rich Strond:
Faire Florimell of Arthure is
Long followed, but not fond.

I
Where is the antique glory now become,
That whylome wont in wemen to appeare?
Where be the brave atchievements doen by some?
Where be the batteilles, where the shield and speare,
And all the conquests which them high did reare,
That matter made for famous poets verse,
And boastfull men so oft abasht to heare?
Beene they all dead, and laide in dolefull herse?
Or doen they onely sleepe, and shall againe reverse?

II
If they be dead, then woe is me therefore:
But if they sleepe, O let them soone awake!
For all too long I burne with envy sore,
To heare the warlike feates which Homere spake
Of bold Penthesilee, which made a lake
Of Greekish blood so ofte in Trojan plaine;
But when I reade, how stout Debora strake
Proud Sisera, and how Camill' hath slaine
The huge Orsilochus, I swell with great disdaine.

III
Yet these, and all that els had puissaunce,
Cannot with noble Britomart compare,
Aswell for glorie of great valiaunce,
As for pure chastitie and vertue rare,
That all her goodly deedes do well declare.
Well worthie stock, from which the branches sprong
That in late yeares so faire a blossome bare
As thee, O Queene, the matter of my song,
Whose lignage from this lady I derive along.

IV
Who when, through speaches with the Redcrosse Knight,
She learned had th' estate of Arthegall,
And in each point her selfe informd aright,
A frendly league of love perpetuall
She with him bound, and congé tooke withall.
Then he forth on his journey did proceede,
To seeke adventures which mote him befall,
And win him worship through his warlike deed,
Which alwaies of his paines he made the chiefest meed.

V
But Britomart kept on her former course,

Ne ever dofte her armes, but all the way
Grew pensive through that amarous discourse,
By which the Redcrosse Knight did earst display
Her lovers shape and chevalrous aray:
A thousand thoughts she fashioned in her mind,
And in her feigning fancie did pourtray
Him such as fittest she for love could find,
Wise, warlike, personable, courteous, and kind.

VI
With such selfe-pleasing thoughts her wound she fedd,
And thought so to beguile her grievous smart;
But so her smart was much more grievous bredd,
And the deepe wound more deep engord her hart,
That nought but death her dolour mote depart.
So forth she rode without repose or rest,
Searching all lands and each remotest part,
Following the guydaunce of her blinded guest,
Till that to the seacoast at length she her addrest.

VII
There she alighted from her light-foot beast,
And sitting downe upon the rocky shore,
Badd her old squyre unlace her lofty creast:
Tho, having vewd a while the surges hore,
That gainst the craggy clifts did loudly rore,
And in their raging surquedry disdaynd
That the fast earth affronted them so sore,
And their devouring covetize restraynd,
Thereat she sighed deepe, and after thus complaynd.

VIII
'Huge sea of sorrow and tempestuous griefe,
Wherein my feeble barke is tossed long,
Far from the hoped haven of reliefe,
Why doe thy cruel billowes beat so strong,
And thy moyst mountaynes each on others throng,
Threatning to swallow up my fearefull lyfe?
O! doe thy cruell wrath and spightfull wrong
At length allay, and stint thy stormy stryfe,
Which in these troubled bowels raignes and rageth ryfe.

IX
'For els my feeble vessell, crazd and crackt
Through thy strong buffets and outrageous blowes,
Cannot endure, but needes it must be wrackt
On the rough rocks, or on the sandy shallowes,
The whiles that Love it steres, and Fortune rowes:
Love, my lewd pilott, hath a restlesse minde,
And Fortune, boteswaine, no assuraunce knowes,
But saile withouten starres gainst tyde and winde:

How can they other doe, sith both are bold and blinde?

X
'Thou god of windes, that raignest in the seas,
That raignest also in the continent,
At last blow up some gentle gale of ease,
The which may bring my ship, ere it be rent,
Unto the gladsome port of her intent:
Then, when I shall my selfe in safety see,
A table, for eternall moniment
Of thy great grace, and my great jeopardee,
Great Neptune, I avow to hallow unto thee.'

XI
Then sighing softly sore, and inly deepe,
She shut up all her plaint in privy griefe;
For her great courage would not let her weepe;
Till that old Glauce gan with sharpe repriefe
Her to restraine, and give her good reliefe,
Through hope of those which Merlin had her told
Should of her name and nation be chiefe,
And fetch their being from the sacred mould
Of her immortall womb, to be in heaven enrold.

XII
Thus as she her recomforted, she spyde
Where far away one, all in armour bright,
With hasty gallop towards her did ryde:
Her dolour soone she ceast, and on her dight
Her helmet, to her courser mounting light:
Her former sorrow into suddein wrath,
Both coosen passions of distroubled spright,
Converting, forth she beates the dusty path:
Love and despight attonce her courage kindled hath.

XIII
As when a foggy mist hath overcast
The face of heven, and the cleare ayre engroste,
The world in darkenes dwels, till that at last
The watry southwinde, from the seabord coste
Upblowing, doth disperse the vapour lo'ste,
And poures it selfe forth in a stormy showre;
So the fayre Britomart, having disclo'ste
Her clowdy care into a wrathfull stowre,
The mist of griefe dissolv'd did into vengeance powre.

XIV
Eftsoones her goodly shield addressing fayre,
That mortall speare she in her hand did take,
And unto battaill did her selfe prepayre.
The knight, approching, sternely her bespake:

'Sir knight, that doest thy voyage rashly make
By this forbidden way in my despight,
Ne doest by others death ensample take,
I read thee soone retyre, whiles thou hast might,
Least afterwards it be too late to take thy flight.'

XV
Ythrild with deepe disdaine of his proud threat,
She shortly thus: 'Fly they, that need to fly;
Wordes fearen babes: I meane not thee entreat
To passe; but maugre thee will passe or dy:'
Ne lenger stayd for th' other to reply,
But with sharpe speare the rest made dearly knowne.
Strongly the straunge knight ran, and sturdily
Strooke her full on the brest, that made her downe
Decline her head, and touch her crouper with her crown.

XVI
But she againe him in the shield did smite
With so fierce furie and great puissaunce,
That through his threesquare scuchin percing quite,
And through his mayled hauberque, by mischaunce
The wicked steele through his left side did glaunce:
Him so transfixed she before her bore
Beyond his croupe, the length of all her launce,
Till, sadly soucing on the sandy shore,
He tombled on an heape, and wallowd in his gore.

XVII
Like as the sacred oxe, that carelesse stands
With gilden hornes and flowry girlonds crownd,
Proud of his dying honor and deare bandes,
Whiles th' altars fume with frankincense arownd,
All suddeinly with mortall stroke astownd,
Doth groveling fall, and with his streaming gore
Distaines the pillours and the holy grownd,
And the faire flowres that decked him afore:
So fell proud Marinell upon the pretious shore.

XVIII
The martiall mayd stayd not him to lament,
But forward rode, and kept her ready way
Along the strond; which as she over-went,
She saw bestrowed all with rich aray
Of pearles and pretious stones of great assay,
And all the gravell mixt with golden owre;
Whereat she wondred much, but would not stay
For gold, or perles, or pretious stones an howre,
But them despised all, for all was in her powre.

XIX

Whiles thus he lay in deadly stonishment,
Tydings hereof came to his mothers eare:
His mother was the blacke-browd Cymoent,
The daughter of great Nereus, which did beare
This warlike sonne unto an earthly peare,
The famous Dumarin; who on a day
Finding the nymph a sleepe in secret wheare,
As he by chaunce did wander that same way,
Was taken with her love, and by her closely lay.

XX
There he this knight of her begot, whom borne
She, of his father, Marinell did name,
And in a rocky cave, as wight forlorne,
Long time she fostred up, till he became
A mighty man at armes, and mickle fame
Did get through great adventures by him donne:
For never man he suffred by that same
Rich Strond to travell, whereas he did wonne,
But that he must do battail with the sea-nymphes sonne.

XXI
An hundred knights of honorable name
He had subdew'd, and them his vassals made,
That through all Farie Lond his noble fame
Now blazed was, and feare did all invade,
That none durst passen through that perilous glade.
And to advaunce his name and glory more,
Her sea-god syre she dearely did perswade,
T' endow her sonne with threasure and rich store,
Bove all the sonnes that were of earthly wombes ybore.

XXII
The god did graunt his daughters deare demaund,
To doen his nephew in all riches flow:
Eftsoones his heaped waves he did commaund
Out of their hollow bosome forth to throw
All the huge threasure, which the sea below
Had in his greedy gulfe devoured deepe,
And him enriched through the overthrow
And wreckes of many wretches, which did weepe
And often wayle their wealth, which he from them did keepe.

XXIII
Shortly upon that shore there heaped was
Exceeding riches and all pretious things,
The spoyle of all the world, that it did pas
The wealth of th' East, and pompe of Persian kings:
Gold, amber, yvorie, perles, owches, rings,
And all that els was pretious and deare,
The sea unto him voluntary brings,

That shortly he a great lord did appeare,
As was in all the lond of Faery, or else wheare.

XXIV
Thereto he was a doughty dreaded knight,
Tryde often to the scath of many deare,
That none in equall armes him matchen might:
The which his mother seeing, gan to feare
Least his too haughtie hardines might reare
Some hard mishap, in hazard of his life:
Forthy she oft him counseld to forbeare
The bloody batteill, and to stirre up strife,
But after all his warre to rest his wearie knife.

XXV
And, for his more assuraunce, she inquir'd
One day of Proteus by his mighty spell
(For Proteus was with prophecy inspir'd)
Her deare sonnes destiny to her to tell,
And the sad end of her sweet Marinell.
Who, through foresight of his eternall skill,
Bad her from womankind to keepe him well:
For of a woman he should have much ill;
A virgin straunge and stout him should dismay or kill.

XXVI
Forthy she gave him warning every day,
The love of women not to entertaine;
A lesson too too hard for living clay,
From love in course of nature to refraine:
Yet he his mothers lore did well retaine,
And ever from fayre ladies love did fly;
Yet many ladies fayre did oft complaine,
That they for love of him would algates dy:
Dy who so list for him, he was loves enimy.

XXVII
But ah! who can deceive his destiny,
Or weene by warning to avoyd his fate?
That, when he sleepes in most security
And safest seemes, him soonest doth amate,
And findeth dew effect or soone or late.
So feeble is the powre of fleshly arme!
His mother bad him wemens love to hate,
For she of womans force did feare no harme;
So weening to have arm'd him, she did quite disarme.

XXVIII
This was that woman, this that deadly wownd,
That Proteus prophecide should him dismay,
The which his mother vainely did expownd,

To be hart-wownding love, which should assay
To bring her sonne unto his last decay.
So ticle be the termes of mortall state
And full of subtile sophismes, which doe play
With double sences, and with false debate,
T' approve the unknowen purpose of eternall fate.

XXIX
Too trew the famous Marinell it fownd,
Who, through late triall, on that wealthy strond
Inglorious now lies in sencelesse swownd,
Through heavy stroke of Britomartis hond.
Which when his mother deare did understand,
And heavy tidings heard, whereas she playd
Amongst her watry sisters by a pond,
Gathering sweete daffadillyes, to have made
Gay girlonds, from the sun their forheads fayr to shade,

XXX
Eftesoones both flowres and girlonds far away
Shee flong, and her faire deawy locks yrent;
To sorrow huge she turnd her former play,
And gamesome merth to grievous dreriment:
Shee threw her selfe downe on the continent,
Ne word did speake, but lay as in a swowne,
Whiles al her sisters did for her lament,
With yelling outcries, and with shrieking sowne;
And every one did teare her girlond from her crowne.

XXXI
Soone as shee up out of her deadly fitt
Arose, shee bad her charett to be brought,
And all her sisters, that with her did sitt,
Bad eke attonce their charetts to be sought:
Tho, full of bitter griefe and pensife thought,
She to her wagon clombe; clombe all the rest,
And forth together went, with sorow fraught.
The waves, obedient to theyr beheast,
Them yielded ready passage, and their rage surceast.

XXXII
Great Neptune stoode amazed at their sight,
Whiles on his broad rownd backe they softly slid,
And eke him selfe mournd at their mournfull plight,
Yet wist not what their wailing ment, yet did,
For great compassion of their sorow, bid
His mighty waters to them buxome bee:
Eftesoones the roaring billowes still abid,
And all the griesly monsters of the see
Stood gaping at their gate, and wondred them to see.

XXXIII
A teme of dolphins, raunged in aray,
Drew the smooth charett of sad Cymoent;
They were all taught by Triton to obay
To the long raynes at her commaundement:
As swifte as swallowes on the waves they went,
That their brode flaggy finnes no fome did reare,
Ne bubling rowndell they behinde them sent;
The rest of other fishes drawen weare,
Which with their finny oars the swelling sea did sheare.

XXXIV
Soone as they bene arriv'd upon the brim
Of the Rich Strond, their charets they forlore,
And let their temed fishes softly swim
Along the margent of the fomy shore,
Least they their finnes should bruze, and surbate sore
Their tender feete upon the stony grownd:
And comming to the place, where all in gore
And cruddy blood enwallowed they fownd
The lucklesse Marinell, lying in deadly swownd;

XXXV
His mother swowned thrise, and the third time
Could scarce recovered bee out of her paine;
Had she not beene devoide of mortall slime,
Shee should not then have bene relyv'd againe;
But soone as life recovered had the raine,
Shee made so piteous mone and deare wayment,
That the hard rocks could scarse from tears refraine,
And all her sister nymphes with one consent
Supplide her sobbing breaches with sad complement.

XXXVI
'Deare image of my selfe,' she sayd, 'that is,
The wretched sonne of wretched mother borne,
Is this thine high advauncement? O! is this
Th' immortall name, with which thee yet unborne
Thy gransire Nereus promist to adorne?
Now lyest thou of life and honor refte,
Now lyest thou a lumpe of earth forlorne,
Ne of thy late life memory is lefte,
Ne can thy irrevocable desteny bee wefte?

XXXVII
'Fond Proteus, father of false prophecis!
And they more fond, that credit to thee give!
Not this the worke of womans hand ywis,
That so deepe wound through these deare members drive.
I feared love: but they that love doe live,
But they that dye doe nether love nor hate.

Nath'lesse to thee thy folly I forgive,
And to my selfe and to accursed fate
The guilt I doe ascribe: deare wisedom bought too late.

XXXVIII
'O what availes it of immortall seed
To beene ybredd and never borne to dye?
Farre better I it deeme to die with speed,
Then waste in woe and waylfull miserye.
Who dyes the utmost dolor doth abye,
But who that lives is lefte to waile his losse:
So life is losse, and death felicity:
Sad life worse then glad death: and greater crosse
To see frends grave, then dead the grave self to engrosse.

XXXIX
'But if the heavens did his dayes envie,
And my short blis maligne, yet mote they well
Thus much afford me, ere that he did die,
That the dim eies of my deare Marinell
I mote have closed, and him bed farewell,
Sith other offices for mother meet
They would not graunt ———
Yett, maulgre them, farewell, my sweetest sweet!
Farewell, my sweetest sonne, sith we no more shall meet!'

XL
Thus when they all had sorowed their fill,
They softly gan to search his griesly wownd:
And that they might him handle more at will,
They him disarmd, and spredding on the grownd
Their watchet mantles frindgd with silver rownd,
They softly wipt away the gelly blood
From th' orifice; which having well upbownd,
They pourd in soveraine balme and nectar good,
Good both for erthly med'cine and for hevenly food.

XLI
Tho, when the lilly handed Liagore
(This Liagore whilome had learned skill
In leaches craft, by great Appolloes lore,
Sith her whilome upon high Pindus hill
He loved, and at last her wombe did fill
With hevenly seed, whereof wise Pæon sprong)
Did feele his pulse, shee knew there staied still
Some litle life his feeble sprites emong;
Which to his mother told, despeyre she from her flong.

XLII
Tho up him taking in their tender hands,
They easely unto her charett beare:

Her teme at her commaundement quiet stands,
Whiles they the corse into her wagon reare,
And strowe with flowres the lamentable beare:
Then all the rest into their coches clim,
And through the brackish waves their passage shear;
Upon great Neptunes necke they softly swim,
And to her watry chamber swiftly carry him.

XLIII
Deepe in the bottome of the sea, her bowre
Is built of hollow billowes heaped hye,
Like to thicke clouds that threat a stormy showre,
And vauted all within, like to the skye,
In which the gods doe dwell eternally:
There they him laide in easy couch well dight,
And sent in haste for Tryphon, to apply
Salves to his wounds, and medicines of might:
For Tryphon of sea gods the soveraine leach is hight.

XLIV
The whiles the nymphes sitt all about him rownd,
Lamenting his mishap and heavy plight;
And ofte his mother, vewing his wide wownd,
Cursed the hand that did so deadly smight
Her dearest sonne, her dearest harts delight.
But none of all those curses overtooke
The warlike maide, th' ensample of that might;
But fairely well shee thryvd, and well did brooke
Her noble deeds, ne her right course for ought forsooke.

XLV
Yet did false Archimage her still pursew,
To bring to passe his mischievous intent,
Now that he had her singled from the crew
Of courteous knights, the Prince and Fary gent,
Whom late in chace of beauty excellent
Shee lefte, pursewing that same foster strong;
Of whose fowle outrage they impatient,
And full of firy zele, him followed long,
To reskew her from shame, and to revenge her wrong.

XLVI
Through thick and thin, through mountains and through playns,
Those two gret champions did attonce pursew
The fearefull damzell, with incessant payns:
Who from them fled, as light-foot hare from vew
Of hunter swifte and sent of howndes trew.
At last they came unto a double way,
Where, doubtfull which to take, her to reskew,
Themselves they did dispart, each to assay
Whether more happy were to win so goodly pray.

XLVII
But Timias, the Princes gentle squyre,
That ladies love unto his lord forlent,
And with proud envy and indignant yre
After that wicked foster fiercely went.
So beene they three three sondry wayes ybent:
But fayrest fortune to the Prince befell;
Whose chaunce it was, that soone he did repent,
To take that way in which that damozell
Was fledd afore, affraid of him as feend of hell.

XLVIII
At last of her far of he gained vew:
Then gan he freshly pricke his fomy steed,
And ever as he nigher to her drew,
So evermore he did increase his speed,
And of each turning still kept wary heed:
Alowd to her he oftentimes did call,
To doe away vaine doubt and needlesse dreed:
Full myld to her he spake, and oft let fall
Many meeke wordes, to stay and comfort her withall.

XLIX
But nothing might relent her hasty flight;
So deepe the deadly feare of that foule swaine
Was earst impressed in her gentle spright:
Like as a fearefull dove, which through the raine
Of the wide ayre her way does cut amaine,
Having farre off espyde a tassell gent,
Which after her his nimble winges doth straine,
Doubleth her hast for feare to bee forhent,
And with her pineons cleaves the liquid firmament.

L
With no lesse hast, and eke with no lesse dreed,
That fearefull ladie fledd from him that ment
To her no evill thought nor evill deed;
Yet former feare of being fowly shent
Carried her forward with her first intent:
And though, oft looking backward, well she vewde
Her selfe freed from that foster insolent,
And that it was a knight which now her sewde,
Yet she no lesse the knight feard then that villein rude.

LI
His uncouth shield and straunge armes her dismayd,
Whose like in Faery Lond were seldom seene,
That fast she from him fledd, no lesse afrayd
Then of wilde beastes if she had chased beene:
Yet he her followd still with corage keene,

So long that now the golden Hesperus
Was mounted high in top of heaven sheene,
And warnd his other brethren joyeous
To light their blessed lamps in Joves eternall hous.

LII
All suddeinly dim wox the dampish ayre,
And griesly shadowes covered heaven bright,
That now with thousand starres was decked fayre;
Which when the Prince beheld, a lothfull sight,
And that perforce, for want of lenger light,
He mote surceasse his suit, and lose the hope
Of his long labour, he gan fowly wyte
His wicked fortune, that had turnd aslope,
And cursed Night, that reft from him so goodly scope.

LIII
Tho, when her wayes he could no more descry,
But to and fro at disaventure strayd,
Like as a ship, whose lodestar suddeinly
Covered with cloudes her pilott hath dismayd,
His wearisome pursuit perforce he stayd,
And from his loftie steed dismounting low,
Did let him forage. Downe himselfe he layd
Upon the grassy ground, to sleepe a throw;
The cold earth was his couch, the hard steele his pillow.

LIV
But gentle Sleepe envyde him any rest;
In stead thereof sad sorow and disdaine
Of his hard hap did vexe his noble brest,
And thousand fancies bett his ydle brayne
With their light wings, the sights of semblants vaine;
Oft did he wish that lady faire mote bee
His Faery Queene, for whom he did complaine;
Or that his Faery Queene were such as shee;
And ever hasty Night he blamed bitterlie.

LV
'Night, thou foule mother of annoyaunce sad,
Sister of heavie Death, and nourse of Woe,
Which wast begot in heaven, but for thy bad
And brutish shape thrust downe to hell below,
Where by the grim floud of Cocytus slow
Thy dwelling is, in Herebus black hous,
(Black Herebus, thy husband, is the foe
Of all the gods) where thou ungratious
Halfe of thy dayes doest lead in horrour hideous:

LVI
'What had th' Eternall Maker need of thee,

The world in his continuall course to keepe,
That doest all thinges deface, ne lettest see
The beautie of his worke? Indeed, in sleepe
The slouthfull body that doth love to steep
His lustlesse limbes, and drowne his baser mind,
Doth praise thee oft, and oft from Stygian deepe
Calles thee, his goddesse in his errour blind,
And great Dame Natures handmaide chearing every kind.

LVII
'But well I wote, that to an heavy hart
Thou art the roote and nourse of bitter cares,
Breeder of new, renewer of old smarts:
In stead of rest thou lendest rayling teares,
In stead of sleepe thou sendest troublous feares
And dreadfull visions, in the which alive
The dreary image of sad death appeares:
So from the wearie spirit thou doest drive
Desired rest, and men of happinesse deprive.

LVIII
'Under thy mantle black there hidden lye
Light-shonning thefte, and traiterous intent,
Abhorred bloodshed, and vile felony,
Shamefull deceipt, and daunger imminent,
Fowle horror, and eke hellish dreriment:
All these, I wote, in thy protection bee,
And light doe shonne, for feare of being shent:
For light ylike is loth'd of them and thee,
And all that lewdnesse love doe hate the light to see.

LIX
'For Day discovers all dishonest wayes,
And sheweth each thing as it is in deed:
The prayses of High God he faire displayes,
And His large bountie rightly doth areed.
Dayes dearest children be the blessed seed
Which Darknesse shall subdue and heaven win:
Truth is his daughter; he her first did breed,
Most sacred virgin, without spot of sinne.
Our life is day, but death with darknesse doth begin.

LX
'O when will Day then turne to me againe,
And bring with him his long expected light?
O Titan, hast to reare thy joyous waine:
Speed thee to spred abroad thy beames bright,
And chace away this too long lingring Night;
Chace her away, from whence she came, to hell:
She, she it is, that hath me done despight:
There let her with the damned spirits dwell,

And yield her rowme to Day, that can it governe well.'

LXI
Thus did the Prince that wearie night outweare
In restlesse anguish and unquiet paine;
And earely, ere the Morrow did upreare
His deawy head out of the ocean maine,
He up arose, as halfe in great disdaine,
And clombe unto his steed. So forth he went,
With heavy looke and lumpish pace, that plaine
In him bewraid great grudge and maltalent:
His steed eke seemd t' apply his steps to his intent.

CANTO V

Prince Arthur heares of Florimell:
Three fosters Timias wound;
Belphebe findes him almost dead,
And reareth out of sownd.

I
Wonder it is to see in diverse mindes
How diversly Love doth his pageaunts play,
And shewes his powre in variable kindes:
The baser wit, whose ydle thoughts alway
Are wont to cleave unto the lowly clay,
It stirreth up to sensuall desire,
And in lewd slouth to wast his carelesse day:
But in brave sprite it kindles goodly fire,
That to all high desert and honour doth aspire.

II
Ne suffereth it uncomely idlenesse
In his free thought to build her sluggish nest;
Ne suffereth it thought of ungentlenesse
Ever to creepe into his noble brest;
But to the highest and the worthiest
Lifteth it up, that els would lowly fall:
It lettes not fall, it lettes it not to rest:
It lettes not scarse this Prince to breath at all,
But to his first poursuit him forward still doth call.

III
Who long time wandred through the forest wyde,
To finde some issue thence, till that at last
He met a dwarfe, that seemed terrifyde
With some late perill, which he hardly past,

Or other accident which him aghast;
Of whom he asked, whence he lately came,
And whether now he traveiled so fast:
For sore he swat, and ronning through that same
Thicke forest, was bescracht, and both his feet nigh lame.

IV
Panting for breath, and almost out of hart,
The dwarfe him answerd: 'Sir, ill mote I stay
To tell the same. I lately did depart
From Faery court, where I have many a day
Served a gentle lady of great sway
And high accompt through out all Elfin Land,
Who lately left the same, and tooke this way:
Her now I seeke, and if ye understand
Which way she fared hath, good sir, tell out of hand.'

V
'What mister wight,' saide he, 'and how arayd?'
'Royally clad,' quoth he, 'in cloth of gold,
As meetest may beseeme a noble mayd;
Her faire lockes in rich circlet be enrold,
A fayrer wight did never sunne behold;
And on a palfrey rydes more white then snow,
Yet she her selfe is whiter manifold:
The surest signe, whereby ye may her know,
Is, that she is the fairest wight alive, I trow.'

VI
'Now certes, swaine,' saide he, 'such one, I weene,
Fast flying through this forest from her fo,
A foule ill favoured foster, I have seene;
Her selfe, well as I might, I reskewd tho,
But could not stay, so fast she did foregoe,
Carried away with wings of speedy feare.'
'Ah, dearest God!' quoth he, 'that is great woe,
And wondrous ruth to all that shall it heare.
But can ye read, sir, how I may her finde, or where?'

VII
'Perdy, me lever were to weeten that,'
Saide he, 'then ransome of the richest knight,
Or all the good that ever yet I gat:
But froward Fortune, and too forward Night,
Such happinesse did, maulgre, to me spight,
And fro me reft both life and light attone.
But, dwarfe, aread what is that lady bright,
That through this forrest wandreth thus alone;
For of her errour straunge I have great ruth and mone.'

VIII

'That ladie is,' quoth he, 'where so she bee,
The bountiest virgin and most debonaire
That ever living eye, I weene, did see;
Lives none this day that may with her compare
In stedfast chastitie and vertue rare,
The goodly ornaments of beautie bright;
And is ycleped Florimell the Fayre,
Faire Florimell, belov'd of many a knight,
Yet she loves none but one, that Marinell is hight.

IX
'A sea-nymphes sonne, that Marinell is hight,
Of my deare dame is loved dearely well;
In other none, but him, she sets delight,
All her delight is set on Marinell;
But he sets nought at all by Florimell:
For ladies love his mother long ygoe
Did him, they say, forwarne through sacred spell.
But fame now flies, that of a forreine foe
He is yslaine, which is the ground of all our woe.

X
'Five daies there be since he (they say) was slaine,
And fowre, since Florimell the court forwent,
And vowed never to returne againe,
Till him alive or dead she did invent.
Therefore, faire sir, for love of knighthood gent
And honour of trew ladies, if ye may
By your good counsell, or bold hardiment,
Or succour her, or me direct the way,
Do one or other good, I you most humbly pray.

XI
'So may ye gaine to you full great renowme
Of all good ladies through the world so wide,
And haply in her hart finde highest rowme,
Of whom ye seeke to be most magnifide:
At least eternall meede shall you abide.'
To whom the Prince: 'Dwarfe, comfort to thee take;
For till thou tidings learne, what her betide,
I here avow thee never to forsake.
Ill weares he armes, that nill them use for ladies sake.'

XII
So with the dwarfe he backe retourn'd againe,
To seeke his lady, where he mote her finde;
But by the way he greatly gan complaine
The want of his good squire, late left behinde,
For whom he wondrous pensive grew in minde,
For doubt of daunger, which mote him betide;
For him he loved above all mankinde,

Having him trew and faithfull ever tride,
And bold, as ever squyre that waited by knights side.

XIII
Who all this while full hardly was assayd
Of deadly daunger, which to him betidd;
For whiles his lord pursewd that noble mayd,
After that foster fowle he fiercely ridd,
To bene avenged of the shame he did
To that faire damzell. Him he chaced long
Through the thicke woods, wherein he would have hid
His shamefull head from his avengement strong,
And oft him threatned death for his outrageous wrong.

XIV
Nathlesse the villein sped himselfe so well,
Whether through swiftnesse of his speedie beast,
Or knowledge of those woods, where he did dwell,
That shortly he from daunger was releast,
And out of sight escaped at the least;
Yet not escaped from the dew reward
Of his bad deedes, which daily he increast,
Ne ceased not, till him oppressed hard
The heavie plague that for such leachours is prepard.

XV
For soone as he was vanisht out of sight,
His coward courage gan emboldned bee,
And cast t' avenge him of that fowle despight,
Which he had borne of his bold enimee.
Tho to his brethren came; for they were three
Ungratious children of one gracelesse syre;
And unto them complayned how that he
Had used beene of that foolehardie squyre:
So them with bitter words he stird to bloodie yre.

XVI
Forthwith themselves with their sad instruments
Of spoyle and murder they gan arme bylive,
And with him foorth into the forrest went,
To wreake the wrath, which he did earst revive
In their sterne brests, on him which late did drive
Their brother to reproch and shamefull flight:
For they had vow'd, that never he alive
Out of that forest should escape their might;
Vile rancour their rude harts had fild with such despight.

XVII
Within that wood there was a covert glade,
Foreby a narrow foord, to them well knowne,
Through which it was uneath for wight to wade,

And now by fortune it was overflowne:
By that same way they knew that squyre unknowne
Mote algates passe; forthy themselves they set
There in await, with thicke woods over growne,
And all the while their malice they did whet
With cruell threats, his passage through the ford to let.

XVIII
It fortuned, as they devized had,
The gentle squyre came ryding that same way,
Unweeting of their wile and treason bad,
And through the ford to passen did assay;
But that fierce foster, which late fled away,
Stoutly foorth stepping on the further shore,
Him boldly bad his passage there to stay,
Till he had made amends, and full restore
For all the damage which he had him doen afore.

XIX
With that, at him a quiv'ring dart he threw,
With so fell force and villeinous despite,
That through his haberjeon the forkehead flew,
And through the linked mayles empierced quite,
But had no powre in his soft flesh to bite:
That stroke the hardy squire did sore displease,
But more that him he could not come to smite;
For by no meanes the high banke he could sease,
But labour'd long in that deepe ford with vaine disease.

XX
And still the foster with his long borespeare
Him kept from landing at his wished will.
Anone one sent out of the thicket neare
A cruell shaft, headed with deadly ill,
And fethered with an unlucky quill:
The wicked steele stayd not, till it did light
In his left thigh, and deepely did it thrill:
Exceeding griefe that wound in him empight,
But more that with his foes he could not come to fight.

XXI
At last, through wrath and vengeaunce making way,
He on the bancke arryvd with mickle payne,
Where the third brother him did sore assay,
And drove at him with all his might and mayne
A forest bill, which both his hands did strayne;
But warily he did avoide the blow,
And with his speare requited him agayne,
That both his sides were thrilled with the throw,
And a large streame of blood out of the wound did flow.

XXII

He, tombling downe, with gnashing teeth did bite
The bitter earth, and bad to lett him in
Into the balefull house of endlesse night,
Where wicked ghosts doe waile their former sin.
Tho gan the battaile freshly to begin;
For nathemore for that spectacle bad
Did th' other two their cruell vengeaunce blin,
But both attonce on both sides him bestad,
And load upon him layd, his life for to have had.

XXIII

Tho when that villayn he aviz'd, which late
Affrighted had the fairest Florimell,
Full of fiers fury and indignant hate,
To him he turned, and with rigor fell
Smote him so rudely on the pannikell,
That to the chin he clefte his head in twaine:
Downe on the ground his carkas groveling fell;
His sinfull sowle, with desperate disdaine,
Out of her fleshly ferme fled to the place of paine.

XXIV

That seeing now the only last of three,
Who with that wicked shafte him wounded had,
Trembling with horror, as that did foresee
The fearefull end of his avengement sad,
Through which he follow should his brethren bad,
His bootelesse bow in feeble hand upcaught,
And therewith shott an arrow at the lad;
Which, fayntly fluttring, scarce his helmet raught,
And glauncing fel to ground, but him annoyed naught.

XXV

With that he would have fled into the wood;
But Timias him lightly overhent,
Right as he entring was into the flood,
And strooke at him with force so violent,
That headlesse him into the foord he sent;
The carcas with the streame was carried downe,
But th' head fell backeward on the continent.
So mischief fel upon the meaners crowne;
They three be dead with shame, the squire lives with renowne.

XXVI

He lives, but takes small joy of his renowne;
For of that cruell wound he bled so sore,
That from his steed he fell in deadly swowne;
Yet still the blood forth gusht in so great store,
That he lay wallowd all in his owne gore.
Now God thee keepe, thou gentlest squire alive,

Els shall thy loving lord thee see no more,
But both of comfort him thou shalt deprive,
And eke thy selfe of honor, which thou didst atchive.

XXVII
Providence hevenly passeth living thought,
And doth for wretched mens reliefe make way;
For loe! great grace or fortune thether brought
Comfort to him that comfortlesse now lay.
In those same woods, ye well remember may
How that a noble hunteresse did wonne,
Shee that base Braggadochio did affray,
And made him fast out of the forest ronne;
Belphœbe was her name, as faire as Phæbus sunne.

XXVIII
She on a day, as shee pursewd the chace
Of some wilde beast, which with her arrowes keene
She wounded had, the same along did trace
By tract of blood, which she had freshly seene
To have besprinckled all the grassy greene;
By the great persue, which she there perceav'd,
Well hoped shee the beast engor'd had beene,
And made more haste, the life to have bereav'd:
But ah! her expectation greatly was deceav'd.

XXIX
Shortly she came whereas that woefull squire,
With blood deformed, lay in deadly swownd:
In whose faire eyes, like lamps of quenched fire,
The christall humor stood congealed rownd;
His locks, like faded leaves fallen to grownd,
Knotted with blood in bounches rudely ran;
And his sweete lips, on which before that stownd
The bud of youth to blossome faire began,
Spoild of their rosy red, were woxen pale and wan.

XXX
Saw never living eie more heavy sight,
That could have made a rocke of stone to rew,
Or rive in twaine: which when that lady bright,
Besides all hope, with melting eies did vew,
All suddeinly abasht shee chaunged hew,
And with sterne horror backward gan to start:
But when shee better him beheld, shee grew
Full of soft passion and unwonted smart:
The point of pitty perced through her tender hart.

XXXI
Meekely shee bowed downe, to weete if life
Yett in his frosen members did remaine;

And feeling by his pulses beating rife
That the weake sowle her seat did yett retaine,
She cast to comfort him with busy paine:
His double folded necke she reard upright,
And rubd his temples and each trembling vaine;
His mayled haberjeon she did undight,
And from his head his heavy burganet did light.

XXXII
Into the woods thenceforth in haste shee went,
To seeke for hearbes that mote him remedy;
For shee of herbes had great intendiment,
Taught of the nymphe, which from her infancy
Her nourced had in trew nobility:
There, whether yt divine tobacco were,
Or panachæa, or polygony,
Shee fownd, and brought it to her patient deare,
Who al this while lay bleding out his hart-blood neare.

XXXIII
The soveraine weede betwixt two marbles plaine
Shee pownded small, and did in peeces bruze,
And then atweene her lilly handes twaine
Into his wound the juice thereof did scruze,
And round about, as she could well it uze,
The flesh therewith shee suppled and did steepe,
T' abate all spasme and soke the swelling bruze,
And after having searcht the intuse deepe,
She with her scarf did bind the wound from cold to keepe.

XXXIV
By this he had sweet life recur'd agayne,
And, groning inly deepe, at last his eies,
His watry eies, drizling like deawy rayne,
He up gan lifte toward the azure skies,
From whence descend all hopelesse remedies:
Therewith he sigh'd, and turning him aside,
The goodly maide ful of divinities
And gifts of heavenly grace he by him spide,
Her bow and gilden quiver lying him beside.

XXXV
'Mercy! deare Lord,' said he, 'what grace is this,
That thou hast shewed to me, sinfull wight,
To send thine angell from her bowre of blis,
To comfort me in my distressed plight?
Angell, or goddesse doe I call thee right?
What service may I doe unto thee meete,
That hast from darkenes me returnd to light,
And with thy hevenly salves and med'cines sweete
Hast drest my sinfull wounds? I kisse thy blessed feete.

XXXVI
Thereat she blushing said: 'Ah! gentle squire,
Nor goddesse I, nor angell, but the mayd
And daughter of a woody nymphe, desire
No service but thy safety and ayd;
Which if thou gaine, I shalbe well apayd.
Wee mortall wights, whose lives and fortunes bee
To commun accidents stil open layd,
Are bownd with commun bond of frailtee,
To succor wretched wights, whom we captived see.'

XXXVII
By this her damzells, which the former chace
Had undertaken after her, arryv'd,
As did Belphœbe, in the bloody place,
And thereby deemd the beast had bene depriv'd
Of life, whom late their ladies arrow ryv'd:
Forthy the bloody tract they followd fast,
And every one to ronne the swiftest stryv'd;
But two of them the rest far overpast,
And where their lady was arrived at the last.

XXXVIII
Where when they saw that goodly boy, with blood
Defowled, and their lady dresse his wownd,
They wondred much, and shortly understood
How him in deadly case theyr lady fownd,
And reskewed out of the heavy stownd.
Eftsoones his warlike courser, which was strayd
Farre in the woodes, whiles that he lay in swownd,
She made those damzels search, which being stayd,
They did him set theron, and forth with them convayd.

XXXIX
Into that forest farre they thence him led,
Where was their dwelling, in a pleasant glade
With mountaines rownd about environed,
And mightie woodes, which did the valley shade,
And like a stately theatre it made,
Spreading it selfe into a spatious plaine;
And in the midst a little river plaide
Emongst the pumy stones, which seemd to plaine
With gentle murmure that his cours they did restraine.

XL
Beside the same a dainty place there lay,
Planted with mirtle trees and laurells greene,
In which the birds song many a lovely lay
Of Gods high praise, and of their loves sweet teene,
As it an earthly paradize had beene:

In whose enclosed shadow there was pight
A faire pavilion, scarcely to be seene,
The which was al within most richly dight,
That greatest princes living it mote well delight.

XLI
Thether they brought that wounded squyre, and layd
In easie couch his feeble limbes to rest.
He rested him a while, and then the mayd
His readie wound with better salves new drest:
Daily she dressed him, and did the best,
His grievous hurt to guarish, that she might,
That shortly she his dolour hath redrest,
And his foule sore reduced to faire plight:
It she reduced, but himselfe destroyed quight.

XLII
O foolish physick, and unfruitfull paine,
That heales up one and makes another wound!
She his hurt thigh to him recurd againe,
But hurt his hart, the which before was sound,
Through an unwary dart, which did rebownd
From her faire eyes and gratious countenaunce.
What bootes it him from death to be unbownd,
To be captived in endlesse duraunce
Of sorrow and despeyre without aleggeaunce?

XLIII
Still as his wound did gather, and grow hole,
So still his hart woxe sore, and health decayd:
Madnesse to save a part, and lose the whole!
Still whenas he beheld the heavenly mayd,
Whiles dayly playsters to his wownd she layd,
So still his malady the more increast,
The whiles her matchlesse beautie him dismayd.
Ah God! what other could he doe at least,
But love so fayre a lady, that his life releast?

XLIV
Long while he strove in his corageous brest,
With reason dew the passion to subdew,
And love for to dislodge out of his nest:
Still when her excellencies he did vew,
Her soveraine bountie and celestiall hew,
The same to love he strongly was constraynd:
But when his meane estate he did revew,
He from such hardy boldnesse was restraynd,
And of his lucklesse lott and cruell love thus playnd.

XLV
'Unthankfull wretch,' said he, 'is this the meed,

With which her soverain mercy thou doest quight?
Thy life she saved by her gratious deed,
But thou doest weene with villeinous despight
To blott her honour and her heavenly light.
Dye rather, dye, then so disloyally
Deeme of her high desert, or seeme so light:
Fayre death it is, to shonne more shame, to dy:
Dye rather, dy, then ever love disloyally.

XLVI
'But if to love disloyalty it bee,
Shall I then hate her, that from deathes dore
Me brought? ah! farre be such reproch fro mee!
What can I lesse doe, then her love therefore,
Sith I her dew reward cannot restore?
Dye rather, dye, and dying doe her serve,
Dying her serve, and living her adore;
Thy life she gave, thy life she doth deserve:
Dye rather, dye, then ever from her service swerve.

XLVII
'But, foolish boy, what bootes thy service bace
To her, to whom the hevens doe serve and sew?
Thou a meane squyre, of meeke and lowly place,
She hevenly borne, and of celestiall hew.
How then? of all Love taketh equall vew:
And doth not Highest God vouchsafe to take
The love and service of the basest crew?
If she will not, dye meekly for her sake:
Dye rather, dye, then ever so faire love forsake.'

XLVIII
Thus warreid he long time against his will,
Till that through weaknesse he was forst at last
To yield himselfe unto the mightie ill:
Which, as a victour proud, gan ransack fast
His inward partes, and all his entrayles wast,
That neither blood in face nor life in hart
It left, but both did quite drye up and blast;
As percing levin, which the inner part
Of every thing consumes and calcineth by art.

XLIX
Which seeing fayre Belphoebe, gan to feare
Least that his wound were inly well not heald,
Or that the wicked steele empoysned were:
Litle shee weend that love he close conceald:
Yet still he wasted, as the snow congeald,
When the bright sunne his beams theron doth beat;
Yet never he his hart to her reveald,
But rather chose to dye for sorow great,

Then with dishonorable termes her to entreat.

L
She, gracious lady, yet no paines did spare,
To doe him ease, or doe him remedy:
Many restoratives of vertues rare
And costly cordialles she did apply,
To mitigate his stubborne malady:
But that sweet cordiall, which can restore
A love-sick hart, she did to him envy;
To him, and to all th' unworthy world forlore,
She did envy that soveraine salve, in secret store.

LI
That daintie rose, the daughter of her morne,
More deare then life she tendered, whose flowre
The girlond of her honour did adorne:
Ne suffred she the middayes scorching powre,
Ne the sharp northerne wind thereon to showre,
But lapped up her silken leaves most chayre,
When so the froward skye began to lowre;
But soone as calmed was the christall ayre,
She did it fayre dispred, and let to florish fayre.

LII
Eternall God, in his almightie powre,
To make ensample of his heavenly grace,
In paradize whylome did plant this flowre;
Whence he it fetcht out of her native place,
And did in stocke of earthly flesh enrace,
That mortall men her glory should admyre.
In gentle ladies breste and bounteous race
Of woman kind it fayrest flowre doth spyre,
And beareth fruit of honour and all chast desyre.

LIII
Fayre ympes of beautie, whose bright shining beames
Adorne the world with like to heavenly light,
And to your willes both royalties and reames
Subdew, through conquest of your wondrous might,
With this fayre flowre your goodly girlonds dight
Of chastity and vertue virginall,
That shall embellish more your beautie bright,
And crowne your heades with heavenly coronall,
Such as the angels weare before Gods tribunall.

LIV
To youre faire selves a faire ensample frame
Of this faire virgin, this Belphebe fayre,
To whom, in perfect love and spotlesse fame
Of chastitie, none living may compayre:

Ne poysnous envy justly can empayre
The prayse of her fresh flowring maydenhead;
Forthy she standeth on the highest stayre
Of th' honorable stage of womanhead,
That ladies all may follow her ensample dead.

LV
In so great prayse of stedfast chastity
Nathlesse she was so courteous and kynde,
Tempred with grace and goodly modesty,
That seemed those two vertues strove to fynd
The higher place in her heroick mynd:
So striving each did other more augment,
And both encrease the prayse of woman kynde,
And both encrease her beautie excellent;
So all did make in her a perfect complement.

CANTO VI

**The birth of fayre Belphoebe and
Of Amorett is told:
The Gardins of Adonis fraught
With pleasures manifold.**

I
Well may I weene, faire ladies, all this while
Ye wonder how this noble damozell
So great perfections did in her compile,
Sith that in salvage forests she did dwell,
So farre from court and royall citadell,
The great schoolmaistresse of all courtesy:
Seemeth that such wilde woodes should far expell
All civile usage and gentility,
And gentle sprite deforme with rude rusticity.

II
But to this faire Belphœbe in her berth
The hevens so favorable were and free,
Looking with myld aspect upon the earth
In th' horoscope of her nativitee,
That all the gifts of grace and chastitee
On her they poured forth of plenteous horne;
Jove laught on Venus from his soverayne see,
And Phœbus with faire beames did her adorne,
And all the Graces rockt her cradle being borne.

III

Her berth was of the wombe of morning dew,
And her conception of the joyous prime,
And all her whole creation did her shew
Pure and unspotted from all loathly crime,
That is ingenerate in fleshly slime.
So was this virgin borne, so was she bred,
So was she trayned up from time to time
In all chaste vertue and true bounti-hed,
Till to her dew perfection she was ripened.

IV
Her mother was the faire Chrysogonee,
The daughter of Amphisa, who by race
A Faerie was, yborne of high degree:
She bore Belphæbe, she bore in like cace
Fayre Amoretta in the second place:
These two were twinnes, and twixt them two did share
The heritage of all celestiall grace;
That all the rest it seemd they robbed bare
Of bounty, and of beautie, and all vertues rare.

V
It were a goodly storie to declare
By what straunge accident faire Chrysogone
Conceiv'd these infants, and how them she bare,
In this wilde forrest wandring all alone,
After she had nine moneths fulfild and gone:
For not as other wemens commune brood
They were enwombed in the sacred throne
Of her chaste bodie, nor with commune food,
As other wemens babes, they sucked vitall blood.

VI
But wondrously they were begot and bred,
Through influence of th' hevens fruitfull ray,
As it in antique bookes is mentioned.
It was upon a sommers shinie day,
When Titan faire his beames did display,
In a fresh fountaine, far from all mens vew,
She bath'd her brest, the boyling heat t' allay;
She bath'd with roses red and violets blew,
And all the sweetest flowres that in the forrest grew:

VII
Till, faint through yrkesome wearines, adowne
Upon the grassy ground her selfe she layd
To sleepe, the whiles a gentle slombring swowne
Upon her fell all naked bare displayd:
The sunbeames bright upon her body playd,
Being through former bathing mollifide,
And pierst into her wombe, where they embayd

With so sweet sence and secret power unspide,
That in her pregnant flesh they shortly fructifide.

VIII
Miraculous may seeme to him that reades
So straunge ensample of conception;
But reason teacheth that the fruitfull seades
Of all things living, through impression
Of the sunbeames in moyst complexion,
Doe life conceive and quickned are by kynd:
So, after Nilus inundation,
Infinite shapes of creatures men doe fynd,
Informed in the mud, on which the sunne hath shynd.

IX
Great father he of generation
Is rightly cald, th' authour of life and light;
And his faire sister for creation
Ministreth matter fit, which, tempred right
With heate and humour, breedes the living wight.
So sprong these twinnes in womb of Chrysogone;
Yet wist she nought thereof, but, sore affright,
Wondred to see her belly so upblone,
Which still increast, till she her terme had full outgone.

X
Whereof conceiving shame and foule disgrace,
Albe her guiltlesse conscience her cleard,
She fled into the wildernesse a space,
Till that unweeldy burden she had reard,
And shund dishonor, which as death she feard:
Where, wearie of long traveill, downe to rest
Her selfe she set, and comfortably cheard;
There a sad cloud of sleepe her overkest,
And seized every sence with sorrow sore opprest.

XI
It fortuned, faire Venus having lost
Her little sonne, the winged God of Love,
Who for some light displeasure, which him crost,
Was from her fled, as flit as ayery dove,
And left her blisfull bowre of joy above;
(So from her often he had fled away,
When she for ought him sharpely did reprove,
And wandred in the world in straunge aray,
Disguiz'd in thousand shapes, that none might him bewray;)

XII
Him for to seeke, she left her heavenly hous,
The house of goodly formes and faire aspects,
Whence all the world derives the glorious

Features of beautie, and all shapes select,
With which High God his workmanship hath deckt;
And searched everie way through which his wings
Had borne him, or his tract she mote detect:
She promist kisses sweet, and sweeter things,
Unto the man that of him tydings to her brings.

XIII
First she him sought in court, where most he us'd
Whylome to haunt, but there she found him not;
But many there she found, which sore accus'd
His falshood, and with fowle infamous blot
His cruell deedes and wicked wyles did spot:
Ladies and lordes she every where mote heare
Complayning, how with his empoysned shot
Their wofull harts he wounded had whyleare,
And so had left them languishing twixt hope and feare.

XIV
She then the cities sought from gate to gate,
And everie one did aske, did he him see?
And everie one her answerd, that too late
He had him seene, and felt the crueltee
Of his sharpe dartes and whot artilleree;
And every one threw forth reproches rife
Of his mischievous deedes, and sayd that hee
Was the disturber of all civill life,
The enimy of peace, and authour of all strife.

XV
Then in the countrey she abroad him sought,
And in the rurall cottages inquir'd,
Where also many plaintes to her were brought,
How he their heedelesse harts with love had fir'd,
And his false venim through their veines inspir'd;
And eke the gentle shepheard swaynes, which sat
Keeping their fleecy flockes, as they were hyr'd,
She sweetly heard complaine both how and what
Her sonne had to them doen; yet she did smile thereat.

XVI
But when in none of all these she him got,
She gan avize where els he mote him hyde:
At last she her bethought, that she had not
Yet sought the salvage woods and forests wyde,
In which full many lovely nymphes abyde,
Mongst whom might be that he did closely lye,
Or that the love of some of them him tyde:
Forthy she thether cast her course t' apply,
To search the secret haunts of Dianes company.

XVII
Shortly unto the wastefull woods she came,
Whereas she found the goddesse with her crew,
After late chace of their embrewed game,
Sitting beside a fountaine in a rew;
Some of them washing with the liquid dew
From of their dainty limbs the dusty sweat
And soyle, which did deforme their lively hew;
Others lay shaded from the scorching heat;
The rest upon her person gave attendance great.

XVIII
She, having hong upon a bough on high
Her bow and painted quiver, had unlaste
Her silver buskins from her nimble thigh,
And her lanck loynes ungirt, and brests unbraste,
After her heat the breathing cold to taste;
Her golden lockes, that late in tresses bright
Embreaded were for hindring of her haste,
Now loose about her shoulders hong undight,
And were with sweet ambrosia all besprinckled light.

XIX
Soone as she Venus saw behinde her backe,
She was asham'd to be so loose surpriz'd,
And woxe halfe wroth against her damzels slacke,
That had not her thereof before aviz'd,
But suffred her so careleslly disguiz'd
Be overtaken. Soone her garments loose
Upgath'ring, in her bosome she compriz'd,
Well as she might, and to the goddesse rose,
Whiles all her nymphes did like a girlond her enclose.

XX
Goodly she gan faire Cytherea greet,
And shortly asked her, what cause her brought
Into that wildernesse for her unmeet,
From her sweete bowres, and beds with pleasures fraught:
That suddein chaung the straung adventure thought.
To whom halfe weeping she thus answered:
That she her dearest sonne Cupido sought,
Who in his frowardnes from her was fled;
That she repented sore to have him angered.

XXI
Thereat Diana gan to smile, in scorne
Of her vaine playnt, and to her scoffing sayd:
'Great pitty sure that ye be so forlorne
Of your gay sonne, that gives ye so good ayd
To your disports: ill mote ye bene apayd!'
But she was more engrieved, and replide:

'Faire sister, ill beseemes it to upbrayd
A dolefull heart with so disdainfull pride;
The like that mine, may be your paine another tide.

XXII
'As you in woods and wanton wildernesse
Your glory sett, to chace the salvage beasts,
So my delight is all in joyfulnesse,
In beds, in bowres, in banckets, and in feasts:
And ill becomes you, with your lofty creasts,
To scorne the joy that Jove is glad to seeke;
We both are bownd to follow heavens beheasts,
And tend our charges with obeisaunce meeke:
Spare, gentle sister, with reproch my paine to eeke.

XXIII
'And tell me if that ye my sonne have heard
To lurke emongst your nimphes in secret wize,
Or keepe their cabins: much I am affeard,
Least he like one of them him selfe disguize,
And turne his arrowes to their exercize:
So may he long him selfe full easie hide:
For he is faire, and fresh in face and guize,
As any nimphe (let not it be envide.)'
So saying, every nimph full narrowly shee eide.

XXIV
But Phœbe therewith sore was angered,
And sharply saide: 'Goe, dame; goe, seeke your boy,
Where you him lately lefte, in Mars his bed:
He comes not here; we scorne his foolish joy,
Ne lend we leisure to his idle toy:
But if I catch him in this company,
By Stygian lake I vow, whose sad annoy
The gods doe dread, he dearly shall abye:
Ile clip his wanton wings, that he no more shall flye.'

XXV
Whom whenas Venus saw so sore displeasd,
Shee inly sory was, and gan relent
What shee had said: so her she soone appeasd
With sugred words and gentle blandishment,
Which as a fountaine from her sweete lips went,
And welled goodly forth, that in short space
She was well pleasd, and forth her damzells sent
Through all the woods, to search from place to place,
If any tract of him or tidings they mote trace.

XXVI
To search the God of Love her nimphes she sent,
Throughout the wandring forest every where:

And after them her selfe eke with her went
To seeke the fugitive both farre and nere.
So long they sought, till they arrived were
In that same shady covert whereas lay
Faire Crysogone in slombry traunce whilere:
Who in her sleepe (a wondrous thing to say)
Unwares had borne two babes, as faire as springing day.

XXVII
Unwares she them conceivd, unwares she bore:
She bore withouten paine that she conceiv'd
Withouten pleasure: ne her need implore
Lucinaes aide: which when they both perceiv'd,
They were through wonder nigh of sence berev'd,
And gazing each on other, nought bespake:
At last they both agreed, her seeming griev'd
Out of her heavie swowne not to awake,
But from her loving side the tender babes to take.

XXVIII
Up they them tooke, eachone a babe uptooke,
And with them carried, to be fostered:
Dame Phæbe to a nymphe her babe betooke,
To be upbrought in perfect maydenhed,
And, of her selfe, her name Belphœbe red:
But Venus hers thence far away convayd,
To be upbrought in goodly womanhed,
And in her litle Loves stead, which was strayd,
Her Amoretta cald, to comfort her dismayd.

XXIX
Shee brought her to her joyous paradize,
Wher most she wonnes, when she on earth does dwell:
So faire a place as Nature can devize:
Whether in Paphos, or Cytheron hill,
Or it in Gnidus bee, I wote not well;
But well I wote by triall, that this same
All other pleasaunt places doth excell,
And called is by her lost lovers name,
The Gardin of Adonis, far renowmd by fame.

XXX
In that same gardin all the goodly flowres,
Wherewith Dame Nature doth her beautify,
And decks the girlonds of her paramoures,
Are fetcht: there is the first seminary
Of all things that are borne to live and dye,
According to their kynds. Long worke it were,
Here to account the endlesse progeny
Of all the weeds that bud and blossome there;
But so much as doth need must needs be counted here.

XXXI
It sited was in fruitfull soyle of old,
And girt in with two walls on either side,
The one of yron, the other of bright gold,
That none might thorough breake, nor overstride:
And double gates it had, which opened wide,
By which both in and out men moten pas;
Th' one faire and fresh, the other old and dride:
Old Genius the porter of them was,
Old Genius, the which a double nature has.

XXXII
He letteth in, he letteth out to wend,
All that to come into the world desire:
A thousand thousand naked babes attend
About him day and night, which doe require
That he with fleshly weeds would them attire:
Such as him list, such as eternall Fate
Ordained hath, he clothes with sinfull mire,
And sendeth forth to live in mortall state,
Till they agayn returne backe by the hinder gate.

XXXIII
After that they againe retourned beene,
They in that gardin planted bee agayne,
And grow afresh, as they had never seene
Fleshly corruption nor mortall payne.
Some thousand yeares so doen they there remayne,
And then of him are clad with other hew,
Or sent into the chaungefull world agayne,
Till thether they retourne, where first they grew:
So like a wheele arownd they ronne from old to new.

XXXIV
Ne needs there gardiner to sett or sow,
To plant or prune: for of their owne accord
All things, as they created were, doe grow,
And yet remember well the mighty word,
Which first was spoken by th' Almighty Lord,
That bad them to increase and multiply:
Ne doe they need with water of the ford
Or of the clouds to moysten their roots dry;
For in themselves eternall moisture they imply.

XXXV
Infinite shapes of creatures there are bred,
And uncouth formes, which none yet ever knew;
And every sort is in a sondry bed
Sett by it selfe, and ranckt in comely rew:
Some fitt for reasonable sowles t' indew,

Some made for beasts, some made for birds to weare,
And all the fruitfull spawne of fishes hew
In endlesse rancks along enraunged were,
That seemd the ocean could not containe them there.

XXXVI
Daily they grow, and daily forth are sent
Into the world, it to replenish more;
Yet is the stocke not lessened nor spent,
But still remaines in everlasting store,
As it at first created was of yore:
For in the wide wombe of the world there lyes,
In hatefull darknes and in deepe horrore,
An huge eternal chaos, which supplyes
The substaunces of Natures fruitfull progenyes.

XXXVII
All things from thence doe their first being fetch,
And borrow matter whereof they are made,
Which, whenas forme and feature it does ketch,
Becomes a body, and doth then invade
The state of life out of the griesly shade.
That substaunce is eterne, and bideth so,
Ne when the life decayes, and forme does fade,
Doth it consume and into nothing goe,
But chaunged is, and often altred to and froe.

XXXVIII
The substaunce is not chaungd nor altered,
But th' only forme and outward fashion;
For every substaunce is conditioned
To chaunge her hew, and sondry formes to don,
Meet for her temper and complexion:
For formes are variable, and decay
By course of kinde and by occasion;
And that faire flowre of beautie fades away,
As doth the lilly fresh before the sunny ray.

XXXIX
Great enimy to it, and to all the rest,
That in the Gardin of Adonis springs,
Is wicked Tyme, who, with his scyth addrest,
Does mow the flowring herbes and goodly things,
And all their glory to the ground downe flings,
Where they do wither and are fowly mard:
He flyes about, and with his flaggy winges
Beates downe both leaves and buds without regard,
Ne ever pitty may relent his malice hard.

XL
Yet pitty often did the gods relent,

To see so faire thinges mard and spoiled quight:
And their great mother Venus did lament
The losse of her deare brood, her deare delight:
Her hart was pierst with pitty at the sight,
When walking through the gardin them she saw,
Yet no'te she find redresse for such despight:
For all that lives is subject to that law:
All things decay in time, and to their end doe draw.

XLI
But were it not, that Time their troubler is,
All that in this delightfull gardin growes
Should happy bee, and have immortall blis:
For here all plenty and all pleasure flowes,
And sweete Love gentle fitts emongst them throwes,
Without fell rancor or fond gealosy:
Franckly each paramor his leman knowes,
Each bird his mate, ne any does envy
Their goodly meriment and gay felicity.

XLII
There is continuall spring, and harvest there
Continuall, both meeting at one tyme:
For both the boughes doe laughing blossoms beare,
And with fresh colours decke the wanton pryme,
And eke attonce the heavy trees they clyme,
Which seeme to labour under their fruites lode:
The whiles the joyous birdes make their pastyme
Emongst the shady leaves, their sweet abode,
And their trew loves without suspition tell abrode.

XLIII
Right in the middest of that paradise
There stood a stately mount, on whose round top
A gloomy grove of mirtle trees did rise,
Whose shady boughes sharp steele did never lop,
Nor wicked beastes their tender buds did crop,
But like a girlond compassed the hight,
And from their fruitfull sydes sweet gum did drop,
That all the ground, with pretious deaw bedight,
Threw forth most dainty odours, and most sweet delight.

XLIV
And in the thickest covert of that shade
There was a pleasaunt arber, not by art,
But of the trees owne inclination made,
Which knitting their rancke braunches part to part,
With wanton yvie twyne entrayld athwart,
And eglantine and caprifole emong,
Fashiond above within their inmost part,
That nether Phoebus beams could through them throng,

Nor Aeolus sharp blast could worke them any wrong.

XLV
And all about grew every sort of flowre,
To which sad lovers were transformde of yore;
Fresh Hyacinthus, Phœbus paramoure
And dearest love,
Foolish Narcisse, that likes the watry shore,
Sad Amaranthus, made a flowre but late,
Sad Amaranthus, in whose purple gore
Me seemes I see Amintas wretched fate,
To whom sweet poets verse hath given endlesse date.

XLVI
There wont fayre Venus often to enjoy
Her deare Adonis joyous company,
And reape sweet pleasure of the wanton boy:
There yet, some say, in secret he does ly,
Lapped in flowres and pretious spycery,
By her hid from the world, and from the skill
Of Stygian gods, which doe her love envy;
But she her selfe, when ever that she will,
Possesseth him, and of his sweetnesse takes her fill.

XLVII
And sooth, it seemes, they say: for he may not
For ever dye, and ever buried bee
In balefull night, where all thinges are forgot;
All be he subject to mortalitie,
Yet is eterne in mutabilitie,
And by succession made perpetuall,
Transformed oft, and chaunged diverslie:
For him the father of all formes they call;
Therfore needs mote he live, that living gives to all.

XLVIII
There now he liveth in eternall blis,
Joying his goddesse, and of her enjoyd:
Ne feareth he henceforth that foe of his,
Which with his cruell tuske him deadly cloyd:
For that wilde bore, the which him once annoyd,
She firmely hath emprisoned for ay,
That her sweet love his malice mote avoyd,
In a strong rocky cave, which is, they say,
Hewen underneath that mount, that none him losen may.

XLIX
There now he lives in everlasting joy,
With many of the gods in company,
Which thether haunt, and with the winged boy
Sporting him selfe in safe felicity:

Who, when he hath with spoiles and cruelty
Ransackt the world, and in the wofull harts
Of many wretches set his triumphes hye,
Thether resortes, and laying his sad dartes
Asyde, with faire Adonis playes his wanton partes.

L
And his trew love, faire Psyche, with him playes,
Fayre Psyche to him lately reconcyld,
After long troubles and unmeet upbrayes,
With which his mother Venus her revyld,
And eke himselfe her cruelly exyld:
But now in stedfast love and happy state
She with him lives, and hath him borne a chyld,
Pleasure, that doth both gods and men aggrate,
Pleasure, the daughter of Cupid and Psyche late.

LI
Hether great Venus brought this infant fayre,
The yonger daughter of Chrysogonee,
And unto Psyche with great trust and care
Committed her, yfostered to bee,
And trained up in trew feminitee:
Who no lesse carefully her tendered
Then her owne daughter Pleasure, to whom shee
Made her companion, and her lessoned
In all the lore of love and goodly womanhead.

LII
In which when she to perfect ripenes grew,
Of grace and beautie noble paragone,
She brought her forth into the worldes vew,
To be th' ensample of true love alone,
And lodestarre of all chaste affection
To all fayre ladies, that doe live on grownd.
To Faery court she came, where many one
Admyrd her goodly haveour, and fownd
His feeble hart wide launched with loves cruel wownd.

LIII
But she to none of them her love did cast,
Save to the noble knight, Sir Scudamore,
To whom her loving hart she linked fast
In faithfull love, t' abide for evermore,
And for his dearest sake endured sore,
Sore trouble of an hainous enimy,
Who her would forced have to have forlore
Her former love and stedfast loialty,
As ye may elswhere reade that ruefull history.

LIV

But well I weene ye first desire to learne
What end unto that fearefull damozell,
Which fledd so fast from that same foster stearne,
Whom with his brethren Timias slew, befell:
That was, to weet, the goodly Florimell,
Who, wandring for to seeke her lover deare,
Her lover deare, her dearest Marinell,
Into misfortune fell, as ye did heare,
And from Prince Arthure fled with wings of idle feare.

CANTO VII

The witches sonne loves Florimell:
She flyes, he faines to dy.
Satyrane saves the Squyre of Dames
From gyaunts tyranny.

I
Like as an hynd forth singled from the heard,
That hath escaped from a ravenous beast,
Yet flyes away of her owne feete afeard,
And every leafe, that shaketh with the least
Murmure of winde, her terror hath encreast;
So fledd fayre Florimell from her vaine feare,
Long after she from perill was releast:
Each shade she saw, and each noyse she did heare,
Did seeme to be the same which she escapt whileare.

II
All that same evening she in flying spent,
And all that night her course continewed:
Ne did she let dull sleepe once to relent,
Nor wearinesse to slack her hast, but fled
Ever alike, as if her former dred
Were hard behind, her ready to arrest:
And her white palfrey, having conquered
The maistring raines out of her weary wrest,
Perforce her carried where ever he thought best.

III
So long as breath and hable puissaunce
Did native corage unto him supply,
His pace he freshly forward did advaunce,
And carried her beyond all jeopardy;
But nought that wanteth rest can long aby:
He, having through incessant traveill spent
His force, at last perforce adowne did ly,

Ne foot could further move. The lady gent
Thereat was suddein strook with great astonishment;

IV
And forst t' alight, on foot mote algates fare,
A traveiler unwonted to such way:
Need teacher her this lesson hard and rare,
That Fortune all in equall launce doth sway,
And mortall miseries doth make her play.
So long she traveild, till at length she came
To an hilles side, which did to her bewray
A litle valley, subject to the same,
All coverd with thick woodes, that quite it overcame.

V
Through the tops of the high trees she did descry
A litle smoke, whose vapour him and light,
Reeking aloft, uprolled to the sky:
Which chearefull signe did send unto her sight
That in the same did wonne some living wight.
Eftsoones her steps she thereunto applyd,
And came at last, in weary wretched plight,
Unto the place, to which her hope did guyde,
To finde some refuge there, and rest her wearie syde.

VI
There in a gloomy hollow glen she found
A little cottage, built of stickes and reedes
In homely wize, and wald with sods around,
In which a witch did dwell, in loathly weedes,
And wilfull want, all carelesse of her needes;
So choosing solitarie to abide,
Far from all neighbours, that her divelish deedes
And hellish arts from people she might hide,
And hurt far off unknowne whom ever she envide.

VII
The damzell there arriving entred in;
Where sitting on the flore the hag she found,
Busie (as seem'd) about some wicked gin:
Who, soone as she beheld that suddein stound,
Lightly upstarted from the dustie ground,
And with fell looke and hollow deadly gaze
Stared on her awhile, as one astound,
Ne had one word to speake, for great amaze,
But shewd by outward signes that dread her sence did daze.

VIII
At last, turning her feare to foolish wrath,
She askt, what devill had her thether brought,
And who she was, and what unwonted path

Had guided her, unwelcomed, unsought.
To which the damzell, full of doubtfull thought,
Her mildly answer'd: 'Beldame, be not wroth
With silly virgin, by adventure brought
Unto your dwelling, ignorant and loth,
That crave but rowme to rest, while tempest overblo'th.'

IX
With that, adowne out of her christall eyne
Few trickling teares she softly forth let fall,
That like to orient perles did purely shyne
Upon her snowy cheeke; and there withall
She sighed soft, that none so bestiall
Nor salvage hart, but ruth of her sad plight
Would make to melt, or pitteously appall;
And that vile hag, all were her whole delight
In mischiefe, was much moved at so pitteous sight;

X
And gan recomfort her in her rude wyse,
With womanish compassion of her plaint,
Wiping the teares from her suffused eyes,
And bidding her sit downe, to rest her faint
And wearie limbs awhile. She nothing quaint
Nor s'deignfull of so homely fashion,
Sith brought she was now to so hard constraint,
Sate downe upon the dusty ground anon,
As glad of that small rest, as bird of tempest gon.

XI
Tho gan she gather up her garments rent,
And her loose lockes to dight in order dew,
With golden wreath and gorgeous ornament;
Whom such whenas the wicked hag did vew,
She was astonisht at her heavenly hew,
And doubted her to deeme an earthly wight,
But or some goddesse, or of Dianes crew,
And thought her to adore with humble spright:
T' adore thing so divine as beauty were but right.

XII
This wicked woman had a wicked sonne,
The comfort of her age and weary dayes,
A laesy loord, for nothing good to donne,
But stretched forth in ydlenesse alwayes,
Ne ever cast his mind to covet prayse,
Or ply him selfe to any honest trade,
But all the day before the sunny rayes
He us'd to slug, or sleepe in slothfull shade:
Such laesinesse both lewd and poore attonce him made.

XIII

He, comming home at undertime, there found
The fayrest creature that he ever saw
Sitting beside his mother on the ground;
The sight whereof did greatly him adaw,
And his base thought with terrour and with aw
So inly smot, that, as one which hath gaz'd
On the bright sunne unwares, doth soone withdraw
His feeble eyne, with too much brightnes daz'd,
So stared he on her, and stood long while amaz'd.

XIV

Softly at last he gan his mother aske,
What mister wight that was, and whence deriv'd,
That in so straunge disguizement there did maske,
And by what accident she there arriv'd:
But she, as one nigh of her wits depriv'd,
With nought but ghastly lookes him answered,
Like to a ghost, that lately is reviv'd
From Stygian shores, where late it wandered;
So both at her, and each at other wondered.

XV

But the fayre virgin was so meeke and myld,
That she to them vouchsafed to embace
Her goodly port, and to their senses vyld
Her gentle speach applyde, that in short space
She grew familiare in that desert place.
During which time the chorle, through her so kind
And courteise use, conceiv'd affection bace,
And cast to love her in his brutish mind;
No love, but brutish lust, that was so beastly tind.

XVI

Closely the wicked flame his bowels brent,
And shortly grew into outrageous fire;
Yet had he not the hart, nor hardiment,
As unto her to utter his desire;
His caytive thought durst not so high aspire:
But with soft sighes and lovely semblaunces
He ween'd that his affection entire
She should aread; many resemblaunces
To her he made, and many kinde remembraunces.

XVII

Oft from the forrest wildings he did bring,
Whose sides empurpled were with smyling red,
And oft young birds, which he had taught to sing
His maistresse praises sweetly caroled;
Girlonds of flowres sometimes for her faire hed
He fine would dight; sometimes the squirrell wild

He brought to her in bands, as conquered
To be her thrall, his fellow servant vild;
All which she of him tooke with countenance meeke and mild.

XVIII
But, past awhile, when she fit season saw
To leave that desert mansion, she cast
In secret wize her selfe thence to withdraw,
For feare of mischiefe, which she did forecast
Might be by the witch or that her sonne compast:
Her wearie palfrey closely, as she might,
Now well recovered after long repast,
In his proud furnitures she freshly dight,
His late miswandred wayes now to remeasure right.

XIX
And earely, ere the dawning day appeard,
She forth issewed, and on her journey went;
She went in perill, of each noyse affeard,
And of each shade that did it selfe present;
For still she feared to be overhent
Of that vile hag, or her uncivile sonne:
Who when, too late awaking, well they kent
That their fayre guest was gone, they both begonne
To make exceeding mone, as they had beene undonne.

XX
But that lewd lover did the most lament
For her depart, that ever man did heare;
He knockt his brest with desperate intent,
And scratcht his face, and with his teeth did teare
His rugged flesh, and rent his ragged heare:
That his sad mother, seeing his sore plight,
Was greatly woe begon, and gan to feare
Least his fraile senses were emperisht quight,
And love to frenzy turnd, sith love is franticke hight.

XXI
All wayes shee sought, him to restore to plight,
With herbs, with charms, with counsel, and with teares,
But tears, nor charms, nor herbs, nor counsell might
Asswage the fury which his entrails teares:
So strong is passion that no reason heares.
Tho, when all other helpes she saw to faile,
She turnd her selfe backe to her wicked leares,
And by her divelish arts thought to prevaile,
To bring her backe againe, or worke her finall bale.

XXII
Eftesoones out of her hidden cave she cald
An hideous beast, of horrible aspect,

That could the stoutest corage have appald;
Monstrous, mishapt, and all his backe was spect
With thousand spots of colours queint elect;
Thereto so swifte that it all beasts did pas:
Like never yet did living eie detect;
But likest it to an hyena was,
That feeds on wemens flesh, as others feede on gras.

XXIII
It forth she cald, and gave it streight in charge,
Through thicke and thin her to poursew apace,
Ne once to stay to rest, or breath at large,
Till her he had attaind, and brought in place,
Or quite devourd her beauties scornefull grace.
The monster, swifte as word that from her went,
Went forth in haste, and did her footing trace
So sure and swiftly, through his perfect sent
And passing speede, that shortly he her overhent.

XXIV
Whom when the fearefull damzell nigh espide,
No need to bid her fast away to flie;
That ugly shape so sore her terrifide,
That it she shund no lesse then dread to die;
And her flitt palfrey did so well apply
His nimble feet to her conceived feare,
That whilest his breath did strength to him supply,
From perill free he her away did beare:
But when his force gan faile, his pace gan wex areare.

XXV
Which whenas she perceiv'd, she was dismayd
At that same last extremity ful sore,
And of her safety greatly grew afrayd:
And now she gan approch to the sea shore,
As it befell, that she could flie no more,
But yield her selfe to spoile of greedinesse:
Lightly she leaped, as a wight forlore,
From her dull horse, in desperate distresse,
And to her feet betooke her doubtfull sickernesse.

XXVI
Not halfe so fast the wicked Myrrha fled
From dread of her revenging fathers hond,
Nor halfe so fast, to save her maydenhed,
Fled fearfull Daphne on th' Ægæan strond,
As Florimell fled from that monster yond,
To reach the sea ere she of him were raught:
For in the sea to drowne her selfe she fond,
Rather then of the tyrant to be caught:
Thereto fear gave her wings, and need her corage taught.

XXVII
It fortuned (High God did so ordaine)
As shee arrived on the roring shore,
In minde to leape into the mighty maine,
A little bote lay hoving her before,
In which there slept a fisher old and pore,
The whiles his nets were drying on the sand:
Into the same shee lept, and with the ore
Did thrust the shallop from the floting strand:
So safety fownd at sea, which she fownd not at land.

XXVIII
The monster, ready on the pray to sease,
Was of his forward hope deceived quight,
Ne durst assay to wade the plerous seas,
But, greedily long gaping at the sight,
At last in vaine was forst to turne his flight,
And tell the idle tidings to his dame:
Yet, to avenge his divelishe despight,
He sett upon her palfrey tired lame,
And slew him cruelly, ere any reskew came.

XXIX
And after having him embowelled,
To fill his hellish gorge, it chaunst a knight
To passe that way, as forth he traveiled:
Yt was a goodly swaine, and of great might,
As ever man that bloody field did fight;
But in vain sheows, that wont yong knights bewitch,
And courtly services tooke no delight,
But rather joyd to bee then seemen sich:
For both to be and seeme to him was labor lich.

XXX
It was to weete the good Sir Satyrane,
That raungd abrode to seeke adventures wilde,
As was his wont, in forest and in plaine:
He was all armd in rugged steele unfilde,
As in the smoky forge it was compilde,
And in his scutchin bore a satyres hedd:
He comming present, where the monster vilde
Upon that milke-white palfreyes carcas fedd,
Unto his reskew ran, and greedily him spedd.

XXXI
There well perceivd he, that it was the horse
Whereon faire Florimell was wont to ride,
That of that feend was rent without remorse:
Much feared he, least ought did ill betide
To that faire maide, the flowre of wemens pride;

For her he dearely loved, and in all
His famous conquests highly magnifide:
Besides, her golden girdle, which did fall
From her in flight, he fownd, that did him sore apall.

XXXII
Full of sad feare and doubtfull agony,
Fiercely he flew upon that wicked feend;
And with huge strokes and cruell battery
Him forst to leave his pray, for to attend
Him selfe from deadly daunger to defend:
Full many wounds in his corrupted flesh
He did engrave, and muchell blood did spend,
Yet might not doe him die, but aie more fresh
And fierce he still appeard, the more he did him thresh.

XXXIII
He wist not how him to despoile of life,
Ne how to win the wished victory,
Sith him he saw still stronger grow through strife,
And him selfe weaker through infirmity:
Greatly he grew enrag'd, and furiously
Hurling his sword away, he lightly lept
Upon the beast, that with great cruelty
Rored and raged to be undcrkept;
Yet he perforce him held, and strokes upon him hept.

XXXIV
As he that strives to stop a suddein flood,
And in strong bancks his violence containe,
Forceth it swell above his wonted mood,
And largely overflow the fruitfull plaine,
That all the countrey seemes to be a maine,
And the rich furrowes flote, all quite fordonne:
The wofull husbandman doth lowd complaine,
To see his whole yeares labor lost so soone,
For which to God he made so many an idle boone:

XXXV
So him he held, and did through might amate:
So long he held him, and him bett so long,
That at the last his fiercenes gan abate,
And meekely stoup unto the victor strong:
Who, to avenge the implacable wrong,
Which he supposed donne to Florimell,
Sought by all meanes his dolor to prolong,
Sith dint of steele his carcas could not quell,
His maker with her charmes had framed him so well.

XXXVI
The golden ribband, which that virgin wore

About her sclender waste, he tooke in hand,
And with it bownd the beast, that lowd did rore
For great despight of that unwonted band,
Yet dared not his victor to withstand,
But trembled like a lambe fled from the pray,
And all the way him followd on the strand,
As he had long bene learned to obay;
Yet never learned he such service till that day.

XXXVII
Thus as he led the beast along the way,
He spide far of a mighty giauntesse,
Fast flying on a courser dapled gray
From a bold knight, that with great hardinesse
Her hard pursewd, and sought for to suppresse:
She bore before her lap a dolefull squire,
Lying athwart her horse in great distresse,
Fast bounden hand and foote with cords of wire,
Whom she did meane to make the thrall of her desire.

XXXVIII
Which whenas Satyrane beheld, in haste
He lefte his captive beast at liberty,
And crost the nearest way, by which he cast
Her to encounter ere she passed by:
But she the way shund nathemore forthy,
But forward gallopt fast; which when he spyde,
His mighty speare he couched warily,
And at her ran: she having him descryde,
Her selfe to fight addrest, and threw her lode aside.

XXXIX
Like as a goshauke, that in foote doth beare
A trembling culver, having spide on hight
An eagle, that with plumy wings doth sheare
The subtile ayre, stouping with all his might,
The quarrey throwes to ground with fell despight,
And to the batteill doth her selfe prepare:
So ran the geauntesse unto the fight;
Her fyrie eyes with furious sparkes did stare,
And with blasphemous bannes High God in peeces tare.

XL
She caught in hand an huge great yron mace,
Where with she many had of life depriv'd;
But ere the stroke could seize his aymed place,
His speare amids her sun-brode shield arriv'd;
Yet nathemore the steele a sonder riv'd,
All were the beame in bignes like a mast,
Ne her out of the stedfast sadle driv'd,
But glauncing on the tempred metall, brast

In thousand shivers, and so forth beside her past.

XLI
Her steed did stagger with that puissaunt strooke,
But she no more was moved with that might,
Then it had lighted on an aged oke;
Or on the marble pillour, that is pight
Upon the top of Mount Olympus hight,
For the brave youthly champions to assay,
With burning charet wheeles it nigh to smite:
But who that smites it mars his joyous play,
And is the spectacle of ruinous decay.

XLII
Yet there with sore enrag'd, with sterne regard
Her dreadfull weapon she to him addrest,
Which on his helmet martelled so hard,
That made him low incline his lofty crest,
And bowd his battred visour to his brest:
Where with he was so stund that he n'ote ryde,
But reeled to and fro from east to west:
Which when his cruell enimy espyde,
She lightly unto him adjoyned syde to syde;

XLIII
And on his collar laying puissaunt hand,
Out of his wavering seat him pluckt perforse,
Perforse him pluckt, unable to withstand,
Or helpe himselfe, and laying thwart her horse,
In loathly wise like to a carrion corse,
She bore him fast away. Which when the knight
That her pursewed saw, with great remorse
He nere was touched in his noble spright,
And gan encrease his speed, as she encreast her flight.

XLIV
Whom when as nigh approching she espyde,
She threw away her burden angrily;
For she list not the batteill to abide,
But made her selfe more light, away to fly:
Yet her the hardy knight pursewd so nye
That almost in the backe he oft her strake:
But still, when him at hand she did espy,
She turnd, and semblaunce of faire fight did make;
But when he stayd, to flight againe she did her take.

XLV
By this the good Sir Satyrane gan wake
Out of his dreame, that did him long entraunce,
And seeing none in place, he gan to make
Exceeding mone, and curst that cruell chaunce,

Which reft from him so faire a chevisaunce:
At length he spyde whereas that wofull squyre,
Whom he had reskewed from captivaunce
Of his strong foe, lay tombled in the myre,
Unable to arise, or foot or hand to styre.

XLVI
To whom approching, well he mote perceive
In that fowle plight a comely personage,
And lovely face, made fit for to deceive
Fraile ladies hart with loves consuming rage,
Now in the blossome of his freshest age:
He reard him up, and loosd his yron bands,
And after gan inquire his parentage,
And how he fell into that gyaunts hands,
And who that was, which chaced her along the lands.

XLVII
Then trembling yet through feare, the squire bespake:
'That geauntesse Argante is behight,
A daughter of the Titans which did make
Warre against heven, and heaped hils on hight,
To scale the skyes, and put Jove from his right:
Her syre Typhoeus was, who, mad through merth,
And dronke with blood of men, slaine by his might,
Through incest her of his owne mother Earth
Whylome begot, being but halfe twin of that berth.

XLVIII
'For at that berth another babe she bore,
To weet, the mightie Ollyphant, that wrought
Great wreake to many errant knights of yore,
And many hath to foule confusion brought.
These twinnes, men say, (a thing far passing thought)
Whiles in their mothers wombe enclosd they were,
Ere they into the lightsom world were brought,
In fleshly lust were mingled both yfere,
And in that monstrous wise did to the world appere.

XLIX
'So liv'd they ever after in like sin,
Gainst natures law and good behaveoure:
But greatest shame was to that maiden twin,
Who, not content so fowly to devoure
Her native flesh, and staine her brothers bowre,
Did wallow in all other fleshly myre,
And suffred beastes her body to deflowre,
So whot she burned in that lustfull fyre:
Yet all that might not slake her sensuall desyre.

L

'But over all the countrie she did raunge,
To seeke young men, to quench her flaming thrust,
And feed her fancy with delightfull chaunge:
Whom so she fittest findes to serve her lust,
Through her maine strength, in which she most doth trust,
She with her bringes into a secret ile,
Where in eternall bondage dye he must,
Or be the vassall of her pleasures vile,
And in all shamefull sort him selfe with her defile.

LI
'Me, seely wretch, she so at vauntage caught,
After she long in waite for me did lye,
And meant unto her prison to have brought,
Her lothsom pleasure there to satisfye;
That thousand deathes me lever were to dye,
Then breake the vow, that to faire Columbell
I plighted have, and yet keepe stedfastly.
As for my name, it mistreth not to tell;
Call me the Squyre of Dames; that me beseemeth well.

LII
'But that bold knight, whom ye pursuing saw
That geauntesse, is not such as she seemd,
But a faire virgin, that in martiall law
And deedes of armes above all dames is deemd,
And above many knightes is eke esteemd,
For her great worth; she Palladine is hight:
She you from death, you me from dread, redeemd.
Ne any may that monster match in fight,
But she, or such as she, that is so chaste a wight.'

LIII
'Her well beseemes that quest,' quoth Satyrane:
'But read, thou Squyre of Dames, what vow is this,
Which thou upon thy selfe hast lately ta'ne?'
'That shall I you recount,' quoth he, 'ywis,
So be ye pleasd to pardon all amis.
That gentle lady whom I love and serve,
After long suit and wearie servicis,
Did aske me how I could her love deserve,
And how she might be sure that I would never swerve.

LIV
'I, glad by any meanes her grace to gaine,
Badd her commaund my life to save or spill.
Eftsoones she badd me, with incessaunt paine
To wander through the world abroad at will,
And every where, where with my power or skill
I might doe service unto gentle dames,
That I the same should faithfully fulfill,

And at the twelve monethes end should bring their names
And pledges, as the spoiles of my victorious games.

LV
'So well I to faire ladies service did,
And found such favour in their loving hartes,
That, ere the yeare his course had compassid,
Thre hundred pledges for my good desartes,
And thrise three hundred thanks for my good partes,
I with me brought, and did to her present:
Which when she saw, more bent to eke my smartes
Then to reward my trusty true intent,
She gan for me devise a grievous punishment:

LVI
'To weet, that I my traveill should resume,
And with like labour walke the world arownd,
Ne ever to her presence should presume,
Till I so many other dames had fownd,
The which, for all the suit I could propownd,
Would me refuse their pledges to afford,
But did abide for ever chaste and sownd.'
'Ah! gentle squyre,' quoth he, 'tell at one word,
How many fowndst thou such to put in thy record?'

LVII
'In deed, sir knight,' said he, 'one word may tell
All that I ever fownd so wisely stayd;
For onely three they were disposd so well,
And yet three yeares I now abrode have strayd,
To fynd them out.' 'Mote I,' then laughing sayd
The knight, 'inquire of thee, what were those three,
The which thy proffred curtesie denayd?
Or ill they seemed sure avizd to bee,
Or brutishly brought up, that nev'r did fashions see.'

LVIII
'The first which then refused me,' said hee,
'Certes was but a common courtisane,
Yet flat refusd to have adoe with mee,
Because I could not give her many a jane.'
(Thereat full hartely laughed Satyrane.)
'The second was an holy nunne to chose,
Which would not let me be her chappellane,
Because she knew, she sayd, I would disclose
Her counsell, if she should her trust in me repose.

LIX
'The third a damzell was of low degree,
Whom I in countrey cottage fownd by chaunce:
Full litle weened I, that chastitee

Had lodging in so meane a maintenaunce;
Yet was she fayre, and in her countenaunce
Dwelt simple truth in seemely fashion.
Long thus I woo'd her with dew observaunce,
In hope unto my pleasure to have won,
But was as far at last, as when I first begon.

LX
'Safe har, I never any woman found,
That chastity did for it selfe embrace,
But were for other causes firme and sound,
Either for want of handsome time and place,
Or else for feare of shame and fowle disgrace.
Thus am I hopelesse ever to attaine
My ladies love, in such a desperate case,
But all my dayes am like to waste in vaine,
Seeking to match the chaste wiht th' unchaste ladies traine.'

LXI
'Perdy,' sayd Satyrane, 'thou Squyre of Dames,
Great labour fondly hast thou hent in hand,
To get small thankes, and therewith many blames,
That may emongst Alcides labours stand.'
Thence backe returning to the former land,
Where late he left the beast he overcame,
He found him not; for he had broke his band,
And was returnd againe unto his dame,
To tell what tydings of fayre Florimell became.

CANTO VIII

The witch creates a snowy lady,
Like to Florimell:
Who, wronged by carle, by Proteus sav'd,
Is sought by Paridell.

I
So oft as I this history record,
My hart doth melt with meere compassion,
To thinke how causelesse of her owne accord
This gentle damzell, whom I write upon,
Should plonged be in such affliction,
Without all hope of comfort or reliefe,
That sure I weene, the hardest hart of stone
Would hardly finde to aggravate her griefe;
For misery craves rather mercy then repriefe.

II
But that accursed hag, her hostesse late,
Had so enranckled her malitious hart,
That she desyrd th' abridgement of her fate,
Or long enlargement of her painefull smart.
Now when the beast, which by her wicked art
Late foorth she sent, she backe retourning spyde,
Tyde with her broken girdle, it a part
Of her rich spoyles, whom he had earst destroyd,
She weend, and wondrous gladnes to her hart applyde.

III
And with it ronning hast'ly to her sonne,
Thought with that sight him much to have reliv'd;
Who thereby deeming sure the thing as donne,
His former griefe with furie fresh reviv'd,
Much more then earst, and would have algates riv'd
The hart out of his brest: for sith her dedd
He surely dempt, himselfe he thought depriv'd
Quite of all hope, wherewith he long had fedd
His foolish malady, and long time had misledd.

IV
With thought whereof, exceeding mad he grew,
And in his rage his mother would have slaine,
Had she not fled into a secret mew,
Where she was wont her sprightes to entertaine,
The maisters of her art: there was she faine
To call them all in order to her ayde,
And them conjure, upon eternall paine,
To counsell her so carefully dismayd,
How she might heale her sonne, whose senses were decayd.

V
By their advise, and her owne wicked wit,
She there deviz'd a wondrous worke to frame,
Whose like on earth was never framed yit,
That even Nature selfe envide the same,
And grudg'd to see the counterfet should shame
The thing it selfe. In hand she boldly tooke
To make another like the former dame,
Another Florimell, in shape and looke
So lively and so like that many it mistooke.

VI
The substance, whereof she the body made,
Was purest snow in massy mould congeald,
Which she had gathered in a shady glade
Of the Riphœan hils, to her reveald
By errant sprights, but from all men conceald:
The same she tempred with fine mercury,

And virgin wex, that never yet was seald,
And mingled them with perfect vermily,
That like a lively sanguine it seemd to the eye.

VII
In stead of eyes, two burning lampes she set
In silver sockets, shyning like the skyes,
And a quicke moving spirit did arret
To stirre and roll them, like a womans eyes:
In stead of yellow lockes, she did devyse,
With golden wyre to weave her curled head;
Yet golden wyre was not so yellow thryse
As Florimells fayre heare: and in the stead
Of life, she put a spright to rule the carcas dead:

VIII
A wicked spright, yfraught with fawning guyle
And fayre resemblance, above all the rest
Which with the Prince of Darkenes fell somewhyle
From heavens blis and everlasting rest:
Him needed not instruct, which way were best
Him selfe to fashion likest Florimell,
Ne how to speake, ne how to use his gest;
For he in counterfesaunce did excell,
And all the wyles of wemens wits knew passing well.

IX
Him shaped thus she deckt in garments gay,
Which Florimell had left behind her late,
That who so then her saw would surely say,
It was her selfe whom it did imitate,
Or fayrer then her selfe, if ought algate
Might fayrer be. And then she forth her brought
Unto her sonne, that lay in feeble state;
Who seeing her gan streight upstart, and thought
She was the lady selfe, whom he so long had sought.

X
Tho, fast her clipping twixt his armes twayne,
Extremely joyed in so happy sight,
And soone forgot his former sickely payne;
But she, the more to seeme such as she hight,
Coyly rebutted his embracement light;
Yet still with gentle countenaunce retain'd
Enough to hold a foole in vaine delight:
Him long she so with shadowes entertain'd,
As her creatresse had in charge to her ordain'd.

XI
Till on a day, as he disposed was
To walke the woodes with that his idole faire,

Her to disport, and idle time to pas
In th' open freshnes of the gentle aire,
A knight that way there chaunced to repaire;
Yet knight he was not, but a boastfull swaine,
That deedes of armes had every in despaire,
Proud Braggadocchio, that in vaunting vaine
His glory did repose, and credit did maintaine.

XII
He, seeing with that chorle so faire a wight,
Decked with many a costly ornament,
Much merveiled thereat, as well he might,
And thought that match a fowle disparagement:
His bloody speare eftesoones he boldly bent
Against the silly clowne, who, dead through feare,
Fell streight to ground in great astonishment:
'Villein,' sayd he, 'this lady is my deare;
Dy, if thou it gainesay: I will away her beare.'

XIII
The fearefull chorle durst not gainesay, nor dooe,
But trembling stood, and yielded him the pray;
Who, finding litle leasure her to wooe,
On Tromparts steed her mounted without stay,
And without reskew led her quite away.
Proud man himselfe then Braggadochio deem'd,
And next to none, after that happy day,
Being possessed of that spoyle, which seem'd
The fairest wight on ground, and most of men esteem'd.

XIV
But when hee saw him selfe free from poursute,
He gan make gentle purpose to his dame,
With termes of love and lewdnesse dissolute;
For he could well his glozing speaches frame
To such vaine uses, that him best became:
But she thereto would lend but light regard,
As seeming sory that she ever came
Into his powre, that used her so hard,
To reave her honor, which she more then life prefard.

XV
Thus as they two of kindnes treated long,
There them by chaunce encountred on the way
An armed knight, upon a courser strong,
Whose trampling feete upon the hollow lay
Seemed to thunder, and did nigh affray
That capons corage: yet he looked grim,
And faynd to cheare his lady in dismay,
Who seemd for feare to quake in every lim,
And her to save from outrage meekely prayed him.

XVI
Fiercely that straunger forward came, and nigh
Approching, with bold words and bitter threat,
Bad that same boaster, as he mote on high,
To leave to him that lady for excheat,
Or bide him batteill without further treat.
That challenge did too peremptory seeme,
And fild his senses with abashment great;
Yet, seeing nigh him jeopardy extreme,
He it dissembled well, and light seemd to esteeme;

XVII
Saying, 'Thou foolish knight! that weenst with words
To steale away that I with blowes have wonne,
And broght throgh points of many perilous swords:
But if thee list to see thy courser ronne,
Or prove thy selfe, this sad encounter shonne,
And seeke els without hazard of thy hedd.'
At those prowd words that other knight begonne
To wex exceeding wroth, and him aredd
To turne his steede about, or sure he should be dedd.

XVIII
'Sith then,' said Braggadochio, 'needes thou wilt
Thy daies abridge, through proofe of puissaunce,
Turne we our steeds, that both in equall tilt
May meete againe, and each take happy chaunce.'
This said, they both a furlongs mountenaunce
Retird their steeds, to ronne in even race:
But Braggadochio with his bloody launce
Once having turnd, no more returnd his face,
But lefte his love to losse, and fled him selfe apace.

XIX
The knight, him seeing flie, had no regard
Him to poursew, but to the lady rode,
And having her from Trompart lightly reard,
Upon his courser sett the lovely lode,
And with her fled away without abode.
Well weened he, that fairest Florimell
It was, with whom in company he yode,
And so her selfe did alwaies to him tell;
So made him thinke him selfe in heven, that was in hell.

XX
But Florimell her selfe was far away,
Driven to great distresse by fortune straunge,
And taught the carefull mariner to play,
Sith late mischaunce had her compeld to chaunge
The land for sea, at randon there to raunge:

Yett there that cruell queene avengeresse,
Not satisfyde so far her to estraunge
From courtly blis and wonted happinesse,
Did heape on her new waves of weary wretchednesse.

XXI
For being fled into the fishers bote,
For refuge from the monsters cruelty,
Long so she on the mighty maine did flote,
And with the tide drove forward carelesly;
For th' ayre was milde, and cleared was the skie,
And all his windes Dan Aeolus did keepe
From stirring up their stormy enmity,
As pittying to see her waile and weepe;
But all the while the fisher did securely sleepe.

XXII
At last when droncke with drowsinesse he woke,
And saw his drover drive along the streame,
He was dismayd, and thrise his brest he stroke,
For marveill of that accident extreame;
But when he saw that blazing beauties beame,
Which with rare light his bote did beautifyre,
He marveild more, and thought he yet did dreame
Not well awakte, or that some extasye
Assotted had his sence, or dazed was his eye.

XXIII
But when her well avizing, hee perceiv'd
To be no vision nor fantasticke sight,
Great comfort of her presence he conceiv'd,
And felt in his old corage new delight
To gin awake, and stir his frosen spright:
Tho rudely askte her, how she thether came.
'Ah!' sayd she, 'father, I note read aright
What hard misfortune brought me to this same;
Yet am I glad that here I now in safety ame.

XXIV
'But thou good man, sith far in sea we bee,
And the great waters gin apace to swell,
That now no more we can the mayn-land see,
Have care, I pray, to guide the cock-bote well,
Least worse on sea then us on land befell.'
Thereat th' old man did nought but fondly grin,
And saide, his boat the way could wisely tell:
But his deceiptfull eyes did never lin
To looke on her faire face, and marke her snowy skin.

XXV
The sight whereof in his congealed flesh

Infixt such secrete sting of greedy lust,
That the drie withered stocke it gan refresh,
And kindled heat, that soone in flame forth brust:
The driest wood is soonest burnt to dust.
Rudely to her he lept, and his rough hand,
Where ill became him, rashly would have thrust;
But she with angry scorne him did with stond,
And shamefully reproved for his rudenes fond.

XXVI

But he, that never good nor maners knew,
Her sharpe rebuke full litle did esteeme;
Hard is to teach an old horse amble trew.
The inward smoke, that did before but steeme,
Broke into open fire and rage extreme;
And now he strength gan adde unto his will,
Forcyng to doe that did him fowle misseeme:
Beastly he threwe her downe, ne car'd to spill
Her garments gay with scales of fish, that all did fill.

XXVII

The silly virgin strove him to withstand,
All that she might, and him in vaine revild:
Shee strugled strongly both with foote and hand,
To save her honor from that villaine vilde,
And cride to heven, from humane helpe exild.
O ye brave knights, that boast this ladies love,
Where be ye now, when she is nigh defild
Of filthy wretch? Well may she you reprove
Of falsehood or of slouth, when most it may behove.

XXVIII

But if that thou, Sir Satyran, didst weete,
Or thou, Sir Peridure, her sory state,
How soone would yee assemble many a fleete,
To fetch from sea that ye at land lost late!
Towres, citties, kingdomes ye would ruinate,
In your avengement and dispiteous rage,
Ne ought your burning fury mote abate;
But if Sir Calidore could it presage,
No living creature could his cruelty asswage.

XXIX

But sith that none of all her knights is nye,
See how the heavens, of voluntary grace
And soveraine favor towards chastity,
Doe succor send to her distressed cace:
So much High God doth innocence embrace.
It fortuned, whilest thus she stifly strove,
And the wide sea importuned long space
With shrilling shriekes, Proteus abrode did rove,

Along the fomy waves driving his finny drove.

XXX
Proteus is shepheard of the seas of yore,
And hath the charge of Neptunes mighty heard,
An aged sire with head all frowy hore,
And sprinckled frost upon his deawy beard:
Who when those pittifull outcries he heard
Through all the seas so ruefully resownd,
His charett swifte in hast he thether steard,
Which, with a teeme of scaly phocas bownd,
Was drawne upon the waves, that fomed him arownd.

XXXI
And comming to that fishers wandring bote,
That went at will, withouten card or sayle,
He therein saw that yrkesome sight, which smote
Deepe indignation and compassion frayle
Into his hart attonce: streight did he hayle
The greedy villein from his hoped pray,
Of which he now did very litle fayle,
And with his staffe, that drives his heard astray,
Him bett so sore, that life and sence did much dismay.

XXXII
The whiles the pitteous lady up did ryse,
Ruffled and fowly raid with filthy soyle,
And blubbred face with teares of her faire eyes:
Her heart nigh broken was with weary toyle,
To save her selfe from that outrageous spoyle:
But when she looked up, to weet what wight
Had her from so infamous fact assoyld,
For shame, but more for feare of his grim sight,
Downe in her lap she hid her face, and lowdly shright.

XXXIII
Her selfe not saved yet from daunger dredd
She thought, but chaung'd from one to other feare:
Like as a fearefull partridge, that is fledd
From the sharpe hauke, which her attached neare,
And fals to ground, to seeke for succor theare,
Whereas the hungry spaniells she does spye,
With greedy jawes her ready for to teare;
In such distresse and sad perplexity
Was Florimell, when Proteus she did see thereby.

XXXIV
But he endevored with speaches milde
Her to recomfort, and accourage bold,
Bidding her feare no more her foeman vilde,
Nor doubt himselfe; and who he was her told.

Yet all that could not from affright her hold,
Ne to recomfort her at all prevayld;
For her faint hart was with the frosen cold
Benumbd so inly, that her wits nigh fayld,
And all her sences with abashment quite were quayld.

XXXV
Her up betwixt his rugged hands he reard,
And with his frory lips full softly kist,
Whiles the cold ysickles from his rough beard
Dropped adowne upon her yvory brest:
Yet he him selfe so busily addrest,
That her out of astonishment he wrought,
And out of that same fishers filthy nest
Removing her, into his charet brought,
And there with many gentle termes her faire besought.

XXXVI
But that old leachour, which with bold assault
That beautie durst presume to violate,
He cast to punish for his hainous fault:
Then tooke he him, yet trembling sith of late,
And tyde behind his charet, to aggrate
The virgin, whom be had abusde so sore:
So drag'd him through the waves in scornfull state,
And after cast him up upon the shore;
But Florimell with him unto his bowre he bore.

XXXVII
His bowre is in the bottom of the maine,
Under a mightie rocke, gainst which doe rave
The roring billowes in their proud disdaine,
That with the angry working of the wave
Therein is eaten out an hollow cave,
That seemes rough masons hand with engines keene
Had long while laboured it to engrave:
There was his wonne, ne living wight was seene,
Save one old nymph, hight Panope, to keepe it cleane.

XXXVIII
Thether he brought the sory Florimell,
And entertained her the best he might,
And Panope her entertaind eke well,
As an immortall mote a mortall wight,
To winne her liking unto his delight:
With flattering wordes he sweetly wooed her,
And offered faire guiftes, t' allure her sight;
But she both offers and the offerer
Despysde, and all the fawning of the flatterer.

XXXIX

Dayly he tempted her with this or that,
And never suffred her to be at rest:
But evermore she him refused flat,
And all his fained kindnes did detest;
So firmely she had sealed up her brest.
Sometimes he boasted that a god he hight;
But she a mortall creature loved best:
Then he would make him selfe a mortall wight;
But then she said she lov'd none but a Faery knight.

XL
Then like a Faerie knight him selfe he drest;
For every shape on him he could endew:
Then like a king he was to her exprest,
And offred kingdoms unto her in vew,
To be his leman and his lady trew:
But when all this he nothing saw prevaile,
With harder meanes he cast her to subdew,
And with sharpe threates her often did assayle,
So thinking for to make her stubborne corage quayle.

XLI
To dreadfull shapes he did him selfe transforme,
Now like a gyaunt, now like to a feend,
Then like a centaure, then like to a storme,
Raging within the waves: thereby he weend
Her will to win unto his wished eend.
But when with feare, nor favour, nor with all
He els could doe, he saw him selfe esteemd,
Downe in a dongeon deepe he let her fall,
And threatned there to make her his eternall thrall.

XLII
Eternall thraldome was to her more liefe,
Then losse of chastitie, or chaunge of love:
Dye had she rather in tormenting griefe,
Then any should of falsenesse her reprove,
Or loosenes, that she lightly did remove.
Most vertuous virgin! glory be thy meed,
And crowne of heavenly prayse with saintes above,
Where most sweet hymmes of this thy famous deed
Are still emongst them song, that far my rymes exceed.

XLIII
Fit song of angels caroled to bee!
But yet what so my feeble Muse can frame,
Shalbe t' advance thy goodly chastitee,
And to enroll thy memorable name
In th' heart of every honourable dame,
That they thy vertuous deedes may imitate,
And be partakers of thy endlesse fame.

Yt yrkes me leave thee in this wofull state,
To tell of Satyrane, where I him left of late.

XLIV
Who having ended with that Squyre of Dames
A long discourse of his adventures vayne,
The which himselfe, then ladies, more defames,
And finding not th' hyena to be slayne,
With that same squyre retourned back agayne
To his first way. And as they forward went,
They spyde a knight fayre pricking on the playne,
As if he were on some adventure bent,
And in his port appeared manly hardiment.

XLV
Sir Satyrane him towardes did addresse,
To weet what wight he was, and what his quest:
And comming nigh, eftsoones he gan to gesse
Both by the burning hart which on his brest
He bare, and by the colours in his crest,
That Paridell it was: tho to him yode,
And him saluting as beseemed best,
Gan first inquire of tydinges farre abrode;
And afterwardes, on what adventure now he rode.

XLVI
Who thereto answering said: 'The tydinges bad,
Which now in Faery court all men doe tell,
Which turned hath great mirth to mourning sad,
Is the late ruine of proud Marinell,
And suddein parture of faire Florimell,
To find him forth: and after her are gone
All the brave knightes, that doen in armes excell,
To savegard her, ywandred all alone;
Emongst the rest my lott (unworthy') is to be one.'

XLVII
'Ah! gentle knight,' said then Sir Satyrane,
'Thy labour all is lost, I greatly dread,
That hast a thanklesse service on thee ta'ne,
And offrest sacrifice unto the dead.
For dead, I surely doubt, thou maist aread
Henceforth for ever Florimell to bee,
That all the noble knights of Maydenhead,
Which her ador'd, may sore repent with mee,
And all faire ladies may for ever sory bee.'

XLVIII
Which wordes when Paridell had heard, his hew
Gan greatly chaung, and seemd dismaid to bee;
Then said: 'Fayre sir, how may I weene it trew,

That ye doe tell in such uncerteintee?
Or speake ye of report, or did ye see
Just cause of dread, that makes ye doubt so sore?
For, perdie, elles how mote it ever bee,
That ever hand should dare for to engore
Her noble blood? The hevens such crueltie abhore.'

XLIX
'These eyes did see, that they will ever rew
To have seene,' quoth he, 'when as a monstrous beast
The palfrey whereon she did travell slew,
And of his bowels made his bloody feast:
Which speaking token sheweth at the least
Her certeine losse, if not her sure decay:
Besides, that more suspicion encreast,
I found her golden girdle cast astray,
Distaynd with durt and blood, as relique of the pray.'

L
'Ay me!' said Paridell, 'the signes be sadd,
And but God turne the same to good sooth say,
That ladies safetie is sore to be dradd:
Yet will I not forsake my forward way,
Till triall doe more certeine truth bewray.'
'Faire sir,' quoth he, 'well may it you succeed:
Ne long shall Satyrane behind you stay,
But to the rest, which in this quest proceed,
My labour adde, and be partaker of their speed.'

LI
'Ye noble knights,' said then the Squyre of Dames,
'Well may yee speede in so praiseworthy payne:
But sith the sunne now ginnes to slake his beames
In deawy vapours of the westerne mayne,
And lose the teme out of his weary wayne,
Mote not mislike you also to abate
Your zealous hast, till morrow next againe
Both light of heven and strength of men relate:
Which if ye please, to yonder castle turne your gate.'

LII
That counsell pleased well; so all yfere
Forth marched to a castle them before;
Where soone arryving, they restrained were
Of ready entraunce, which ought evermore
To errant knights be commune: wondrous sore
Thereat displeasd they were, till that young squyre
Gan them informe the cause why that same dore
Was shut to all which lodging did desyre:
The which to let you weet will further time requyre.

CANTO IX

Malbecco will no straunge knights host,
For peevish gealosy:
Paridell giusts with Britomart:
Both shew their auncestry.

I

Redoubted knights, and honorable dames,
To whom I levell all my labours end,
Right sore I feare, least with unworthie blames
This odious argument my rymes should shend,
Or ought your goodly patience offend,
Whiles of a wanton lady I doe write,
Which with her loose incontinence doth blend
The shyning glory of your soveraine light;
And knighthood fowle defaced by a faithlesse knight.

II

But never let th' ensample of the bad
Offend the good: for good, by paragone
Of evill, may more notably be rad,
As white seemes fayrer, macht with blacke attone;
Ne all are shamed by the fault of one:
For lo! in heven, whereas all goodnes is,
Emongst the angels, a whole legione
Of wicked sprightes did fall from happy blis;
What wonder then, if one of women all did mis?

III

Then listen, lordings, if ye list to weet
The cause why Satyrane and Paridell
Mote not be entertaynd, as seemed meet,
Into that castle (as that squyre does tell.)
'Therein a cancred crabbed carle does dwell,
That has no skill of court nor courtesie,
Ne cares what men say of him ill or well;
For all his dayes he drownes in privitie,
Yet has full large to live, and spend at libertie.

IV

'But all his mind is set on mucky pelfe,
To hoord up heapes of evill gotten masse,
For which he others wrongs and wreckes himselfe;
Yet is he lincked to a lovely lasse,
Whose beauty doth her bounty far surpasse,
The which to him both far unequall yeares

And also far unlike conditions has;
For she does joy to play emongst her peares,
And to be free from hard restraynt and gealous feares.

V
'But he is old, and withered like hay,
Unfit faire ladies service to supply,
The privie guilt whereof makes him alway
Suspect her truth, and keepe continuall spy
Upon her with his other blincked eye;
Ne suffreth he resort of living wight
Approch to her, ne keepe her company,
But in close bowre her mewes from all mens sight,
Depriv'd of kindly joy and naturall delight.

VI
'Malbecco he, and Hellenore she hight,
Unfitly yokt together in one teeme:
That is the cause why never any knight
Is suffred here to enter, but he seeme
Such as no doubt of him he neede misdeeme.'
Thereat Sir Satyrane gan smyle, and say:
'Extremely mad the man I surely deeme,
That weenes with watch and hard restraynt to stay
A womans will, which is disposd to go astray.

VII
'In vaine he feares that which he cannot shonne:
For who wotes not, that womans subtiltyes
Can guylen Argus, when she list misdonne?
It is not yron bandes, nor hundred eyes,
Nor brasen walls, nor many wakefull spyes,
That can withhold her wilfull wandring feet;
But fast goodwill with gentle courtesyes,
And timely service to her pleasures meet,
May her perhaps containe, that else would algates fleet.'

VIII
'Then is he not more mad,' sayd Paridell,
'That hath himselfe unto such service sold,
In dolefull thraldome all his dayes to dwell?
For sure a foole I doe him firmely hold,
That loves his fetters, though they were of gold.
But why doe wee devise of others ill,
Whyles thus we suffer this same dotard old
To keepe us out, in scorne, of his owne will,
And rather do not ransack all, and him selfe kill?'

IX
'Nay, let us first,' sayd Satyrane, 'entreat
The man by gentle meanes, to let us in;

And afterwardes affray with cruell threat,
Ere that we to efforce it doe begin:
Then if all fayle, we will by force it win,
And eke reward the wretch for his mesprise,
As may be worthy of his haynous sin.'
That counsell pleasd: then Paridell did rise,
And to the castle gate approcht in quiet wise.

X
Whereat soft knocking, entrance he desyrd.
The good man selfe, which then the porter playd,
Him answered, that all were now retyrd
Unto their rest, and all the keyes convayd
Unto their maister, who in bed was layd,
That none him durst awake out of his dreme;
And therefore them of patience gently prayd.
Then Paridell began to chaunge his theme,
And threatned him with force and punishment extreme.

XI
But all in vaine; for nought mote him relent:
And now so long before the wicket fast
They wayted, that the night was forward spent,
And the faire welkin, fowly overcast,
Gan blowen up a bitter stormy blast,
With showre and hayle so horrible and dred,
That this faire many were compeld at last
To fly for succour to a little shed,
The which beside the gate for swyne was ordered.

XII
It fortuned, soone after they were gone,
Another knight, whom tempest thether brought,
Came to that castle, and with earnest mone,
Like as the rest, late entrance deare besought;
But like so as the rest, he prayd for nought,
For flatly he of entrance was refusd.
Sorely thereat he was displeasd, and thought
How to avenge himselfe so sore abusd,
And evermore the carle of courtesie accusd.

XIII
But to avoyde th' intollerable stowre,
He was compeld to seeke some refuge neare,
And to that shed, to shrowd him from the showre,
He came, which full of guests he found whyleare,
So as he was not let to enter there:
Whereat he gan to wex exceeding wroth,
And swore that he would lodge with them yfere,
Or them dislodg, all were they liefe or loth;
And so defyde them each, and so defyde them both.

XIV
Both were full loth to leave that needfull tent,
And both full loth in darkenesse to debate;
Yet both full liefe him lodging to have lent,
And both full liefe his boasting to abate;
But chiefely Paridell his hart did grate,
To heare him threaten so despightfully,
As if he did a dogge in kenell rate,
That durst not barke; and rather had he dy
Then, when he was defyde, in coward corner ly.

XV
Tho, hastily remounting to his steed,
He forth issew'd; like as a boystrous winde,
Which in th' earthes hollow caves hath long ben hid,
And shut up fast within her prisons blind,
Makes the huge element, against her kinde,
To move and tremble as it were aghast,
Untill that it an issew forth may finde;
Then forth it breakes, and with his furious blast
Confounds both land and seas, and skyes doth overcast.

XVI
Their steel-hed speares they strongly coucht, and met
Together with impetuous rage and forse,
That with the terrour of their fierce affret,
They rudely drove to ground both man and horse,
That each awhile lay like a sencelesse corse.
But Paridell, sore brused with the blow,
Could not arise, the counterchaunge to scorse,
Till that young squyre him reared from below;
Then drew he his bright sword, and gan about him throw.

XVII
But Satyrane, forth stepping, did them stay,
And with faire treaty pacifide their yre:
Then, when they were accorded from the fray,
Against that castles lord they gan conspire,
To heape on him dew vengeaunce for his hire.
They beene agreed, and to the gates they goe,
To burne the same with unquenchable fire,
And that uncurteous carle, their commune foe,
To doe fowle death to die, or wrap in grievous woe.

XVIII
Malbecco seeing them resolvd in deed
To flame the gates, and hearing them to call
For fire in earnest, ran with fearfull speed,
And to them calling from the castle wall,
Besought them humbly him to beare with all,

As ignorant of servants bad abuse,
And slacke attendaunce unto straungers call.
The knights were willing all things to excuse,
Though nought belev'd, and entraunce late did not refuse.

XIX
They beene ybrought into a comely bowre,
And servd of all things that mote needfull bee;
Yet secretly their hoste did on them lowre,
And welcomde more for feare then charitee;
But they dissembled what they did not see,
And welcomed themselves. Each gan undight
Their garments wett, and weary armour free,
To dry them selves by Vulcanes flaming light,
And eke their lately bruzed parts to bring in plight.

XX
And eke that straunger knight emongst the rest
Was for like need enforst to disaray:
Tho, whenas vailed was her lofty crest,
Her golden locks, that were in tramells gay
Upbounden, did them selves adowne display,
And raught unto her heeles; like sunny beames,
That in a cloud their light did long time stay,
Their vapour vaded, shewe their golden gleames,
And through the persant aire shoote forth their azure streames.

XXI
Shee also dofte her heavy haberjeon,
Which the faire feature of her limbs did hyde,
And her well plighted frock, which she did won
To tucke about her short, when she did ryde,
Shee low let fall, that flowd from her lanck syde
Downe to her foot with carelesse modestee.
Then of them all she plainly was espyde
To be a woman wight, unwist to bee,
The fairest woman wight that ever eie did see.

XXII
Like as Minerva, being late returnd
From slaughter of the giaunts conquered;
Where proud Encelade, whose wide nosethrils burnd
With breathed flames, like to a furnace redd,
Transfixed with her speare, downe tombled dedd
From top of Hemus, by him heaped hye;
Hath loosd her helmet from her lofty hedd,
And her Gorgonian shield gins to untye
From her lefte arme, to rest in glorious victorye.

XXIII
Which whenas they beheld, they smitten were

With great amazement of so wondrous sight,
And each on other, and they all on her,
Stood gazing, as if suddein great affright
Had them surprizd. At last avizing right
Her goodly personage and glorious hew,
Which they so much mistooke, they tooke delight
In their first error, and yett still anew
With wonder of her beauty fed their hongry vew.

XXIV
Yet note their hongry vew be satisfide,
But seeing, still the more desir'd to see,
And ever firmely fixed did abide
In contemplation of divinitee:
But most they mervaild at her chevalree
And noble prowesse, which they had approv'd,
That much they faynd to know who she mote bee;
Yet none of all them her thereof amov'd,
Yet every one her likte, and every one her lov'd.

XXV
And Paridell, though partly discontent
With his late fall and fowle indignity,
Yet was soone wonne his malice to relent,
Through gratious regard of her faire eye,
And knightly worth, which he too late did try,
Yet tried did adore. Supper was dight;
Then they Malbecco prayd of courtesy,
That of his lady they might have the sight,
And company at meat, to doe them more delight.

XXVI
But he, to shifte their curious request,
Gan causen why she could not come in place;
Her crased helth, her late recourse to rest,
And humid evening, ill for sicke folkes cace;
But none of those excuses could take place,
Ne would they eate, till she in presence came.
Shee came in presence with right comely grace,
And fairely them saluted, as became,
And shewd her selfe in all a gentle courteous dame.

XXVII
They sate to meat, and Satyrane his chaunce
Was her before, and Paridell beside;
But he him selfe sate looking still askaunce
Gainst Britomart, and ever closely eide
Sir Satyrane, that glaunces might not glide:
But his blinde eie, that sided Paridell,
All his demeasnure from his sight did hide:
On her faire face so did he feede his fill,

And sent close messages of love to her at will.

XXVIII
And ever and anone, when none was ware,
With speaking lookes, that close embassage bore,
He rov'd at her, and told his secret care:
For all that art he learned had of yore.
Ne was she ignoraunt of that leud lore,
But in his eye his meaning wisely redd,
And with the like him aunswerd evermore:
Shee sent at him one fyrie dart, whose hedd
Empoisned was with privy lust and gealous dredd.

XXIX
He from that deadly throw made no defence,
But to the wound his weake heart opened wyde:
The wicked engine through false influence
Past through his eies, and secretly did glyde
Into his heart, which it did sorely gryde.
But nothing new to him was that same paine,
Ne paine at all; for he so ofte had tryde
The powre thereof, and lov'd so oft in vaine,
That thing of course he counted, love to entertaine.

XXX
Thenceforth to her he sought to intimate
His inward griefe, by meanes to him well knowne:
Now Bacchus fruit out of the silver plate
He on the table dasht, as overthrowne,
Or of the fruitfull liquor overflowne,
And by the dauncing bubbles did divine,
Or therein write to lett his love be showne;
Which well she redd out of the learned line:
A sacrament prophane in mistery of wine.

XXXI
And when so of his hand the pledge she raught,
The guilty cup she fained to mistake,
And in her lap did shed her idle draught,
Shewing desire her inward flame to slake.
By such close signes they secret way did make
Unto their wils, and one eies watch escape:
Two eies him needeth, for to watch and wake,
Who lovers will deceive. Thus was the ape,
By their faire handling, put into Malbeccoes cape.

XXXII
Now when of meats and drinks they had their fill,
Purpose was moved by that gentle dame
Unto those knights adventurous, to tell
Of deeds of armes which unto them became,

And every one his kindred and his name.
Then Paridell, in whom a kindly pride
Of gratious speach and skill his words to frame
Abounded, being glad of so fitte tide
Him to commend to her, thus spake, of al well eide:

XXXIII
'Troy, that art now nought but an idle name,
And in thine ashes buried low dost lie,
Though whilome far much greater then thy fame,
Before that angry gods and cruell skie
Upon thee heapt a direfull destinie,
What boots it boast thy glorious descent,
And fetch from heven thy great genealogie,
Sith all thy worthie prayses being blent,
Their ofspring hath embaste, and later glory shent?

XXXIV
'Most famous worthy of the world, by whome
That warre was kindled which did Troy inflame,
And stately towres of Ilion whilome
Brought unto balefull ruine, was by name
Sir Paris, far renowmd through noble fame;
Who, through great prowesse and bold hardinesse,
From Lacedæmon fetcht the fayrest dame,
That ever Greece did boast, or knight possesse,
Whom Venus to him gave for meed of worthinesse:

XXXV
'Fayre Helene, flowre of beautie excellent,
And girlond of the mighty conquerours,
That madest many ladies deare lament
The heavie losse of their brave paramours,
Which they far off beheld from Trojan toures,
And saw the fieldes of faire Scamander strowne
With carcases of noble warrioures,
Whose fruitlesse lives were under furrow sowne,
And Xanthus sandy bankes with blood all overflowne.

XXXVI
'From him my linage I derive aright,
Who long before the ten yeares siege of Troy,
Whiles yet on Ida he a shepeheard hight,
On faire Oenone got a lovely boy,
Whom, for remembrance of her passed joy,
She of his father Parius did name;
Who, after Greekes did Priams realme destroy,
Gathred the Trojan reliques sav'd from flame,
And with them sayling thence, to th' isle of Paros came.

XXXVII

'That was by him cald Paros, which before
Hight Nausa; there he many yeares did raine,
And built Nausicle by the Pontick shore,
The which he dying lefte next in remaine
To Paridas his sonne,
From whom I, Paridell, by kin descend;
But, for faire ladies love and glories gaine,
My native soile have lefte, my dayes to spend
In seewing deeds of armes, my lives and labors end.'

XXXVIII
Whenas the noble Britomart heard tell
Of Trojan warres and Priams citie sackt,
The ruefull story of Sir Paridell,
She was empassiond at that piteous act,
With zelous envy of Greekes cruell fact
Against that nation, from whose race of old
She heard that she was lineally extract:
For noble Britons sprong from Trojans bold,
And Troynovant was built of old Troyes ashes cold.

XXXIX
Then sighing soft awhile, at last she thus:
'O lamentable fall of famous towne,
Which raignd so many yeares victorious,
And of all Asie bore the soveraine crowne,
In one sad night consumd and throwen downe!
What stony hart, that heares thy haplesse fate,
Is not empierst with deepe compassiowne,
And makes ensample of mans wretched state,
That floures so fresh at morne, and fades at evening late?

XL
'Behold, sir, how your pitifull complaint
Hath fownd another partner of your payne:
For nothing may impresse so deare constraint,
As countries cause and commune foes disdayne.
But if it should not grieve you, backe agayne
To turne your course, I would to heare desyre
What to Aeneas fell; sith that men sayne
He was not in the cities wofull fyre
Consum'd, but did him selfe to safety retyre.'

XLI
'Anchyses sonne, begott of Venus fayre,'
Said he, 'out of the flames for safegard fled,
And with a remnant did to sea repayre,
Where he through fatall errour long was led
Full many yeares, and weetlesse wandered
From shore to shore, emongst the Lybick sandes,
Ere rest he fownd. Much there he suffered,

And many perilles past in forreine landes,
To save his people sad from victours vengefull handes.

XLII
'At last in Latium he did arryve,
Where he with cruell warre was entertaind
Of th' inland folke, which sought him backe to drive,
Till he with old Latinus was constraind
To contract wedlock; (so the Fates ordaind;)
Wedlocke contract in blood, and eke in blood
Accomplished, that many deare complaind:
The rivall slaine, the victour, through the flood
Escaped hardly, hardly praisd his wedlock good.

XLIII
'Yet after all, he victour did survive,
And with Latinus did the kingdom part.
But after, when both nations gan to strive,
Into their names the title to convart,
His sonne Iülus did from thence depart
With all the warlike youth of Trojans bloud,
And in Long Alba plast his throne apart,
Where faire it florished, and long time stoud,
Till Romulus, renewing it, to Rome remoud.'

XLIV
'There, there,' said Britomart, 'a fresh appeard
The glory of the later world to spring,
And Troy againe out of her dust was reard,
To sitt in second seat of soveraine king
Of all the world under her governing.
But a third kingdom yet is to arise
Out of the Trojans scattered ofspring,
That, in all glory and great enterprise,
Both first and second Troy shall dare to equalise.

XLV
'It Troynovant is hight, that with the waves
Of wealthy Thamis washed is along,
Upon whose stubborne neck, whereat he raves
With roring rage, and sore him selfe does throng,
That all men feare to tempt his billowes strong,
She fastned hath her foot, which standes so hy,
That it a wonder of the world is song
In forreine landes, and all which passen by,
Beholding it from farre, doe thinke it threates the skye.

XLVI
'The Trojan Brute did first that citie fownd,
And Hygate made the meare thereof by west,
And Overt gate by north: that is the bownd

Toward the land; two rivers bownd the rest.
So huge a scope at first him seemed best,
To be the compasse of his kingdomes seat:
So huge a mind could not in lesser rest,
Ne in small meares containe his glory great,
That Albion had conquered first by warlike feat.'

XLVII
'Ah! fairest lady knight,' said Paridell,
'Pardon, I pray, my heedlesse oversight,
Who had forgot that whylome I hard tell
From aged Mnemon; for my wits beene light.
Indeed he said (if I remember right)
That of the antique Trojan stocke there grew
Another plant, that raught to wondrous hight,
And far abroad his mightie braunches threw
Into the utmost angle of the world he knew.

XLVIII
'For that same Brute, whom much he did advaunce
In all his speach, was Sylvius his sonne,
Whom having slain through luckles arrowes glaunce,
He fled for feare of that he had misdonne,
Or els for shame, so fowle reproch to shonne,
And with him ledd to sea an youthly trayne,
Where wearie wandring they long time did wonne,
And many fortunes prov'd in th' ocean mayne,
And great adventures found, that now were long to sayne.

XLIX
'At last by fatall course they drive were
Into an island spatious and brode,
The furthest north that did to them appeare:
Which, after rest, they seeking farre abrode,
Found it the fittest soyle for their abode,
Fruitfull of all thinges fitt for living foode,
But wholy waste and void of peoples trode,
Save an huge nation of the geaunts broode,
That fed on living flesh, and dronck mens vitall blood.

L
'Whom he, through wearie wars and labours long,
Subdewd with losse of many Britons bold:
In which the great Goemagot of strong
Corineus, and Coulin of Debon old,
Were overthrowne and laide on th' earth full cold,
Which quaked under their so hideous masse:
A famous history to bee enrold
In everlasting moniments of brasse,
That all the antique worthies merits far did passe.

LI
'His worke great Troynovant, his worke is eke
Faire Lincolne, both renowmed far away,
That who from east to west will endlong seeke,
Cannot two fairer cities find this day,
Except Cleopolis: so heard I say
Old Mnemon. Therefore, sir, I greet you well,
Your countrey kin, and you entyrely pray
Of pardon for the strife which late befell
Betwixt us both unknowne.' So ended Paridell.

LII
But all the while that he these speeches spent,
Upon his lips hong faire Dame Hellenore,
With vigilant regard and dew attent,
Fashioning worldes of fancies evermore
In her fraile witt, that now her quite forlore:
The whiles unwares away her wondring eye
And greedy eares her weake hart from her bore:
Which he perceiving, ever privily,
In speaking, many false belgardes at her let fly.

LIII
So long these knightes discoursed diversly
Of straunge affaires, and noble hardiment,
Which they had past with mickle jeopardy,
That now the humid night was farforth spent,
And hevenly lampes were halfendeale ybrent:
Which th' old man seeing wel, who too long thought
Every discourse and every argument,
Which by the houres he measured, besought
Them go to rest. So all unto their bowres were brought.

CANTO X

Paridell rapeth Hellenore:
Malbecco her poursewes:
Fynds emongst Satyres, whence with him
To turne she doth refuse.

I
The morrow next, so soone as Phœbus lamp
Bewrayed had the world with early light,
And fresh Aurora had the shady damp
Out of the goodly heven amoved quight,
Faire Britomart and that same Faery knight
Uprose, forth on their journey for to wend:

But Paridell complaynd, that his late fight
With Britomart so sore did him offend,
That ryde he could not, till his hurts he did amend.

II
So foorth they far'd, but he behind them stayd,
Maulgre his host, who grudged grivously
To house a guest that would be needes obayd,
And of his owne him left not liberty:
Might wanting measure moveth surquedry.
Two things he feared, but the third was death:
That fiers youngmans unruly maystery;
His money, which he lov'd as living breath;
And his faire wife, whom honest long he kept uneath.

III
But patience perforce, he must abie
What fortune and his fate on him will lay;
Fond is the feare that findes no remedie;
Yet warily he watcheth every way,
By which he feareth evill happen may:
So th' evill thinkes by watching to prevent;
Ne doth he suffer her, nor night nor day,
Out of his sight her selfe once to absent.
So doth he punish her and eke himselfe torment.

IV
But Paridell kept better watch then hee,
A fit occasion for his turne to finde.
False Love, why do men say thou canst not see,
And in their foolish fancy feigne thee blinde,
That with thy charmes the sharpest sight doest binde,
And to thy will abuse? Thou walkest free,
And seest every secret of the minde;
Thou seest all, yet none at all sees thee;
All that is by the working of thy deitee.

V
So perfect in that art was Paridell,
That he Malbeccoes halfen eye did wyle;
His halfen eye he wiled wondrous well,
And Hellenors both eyes did eke beguyle,
Both eyes and hart attonce, during the whyle
That he there sojourned his woundes to heale;
That Cupid selfe, it seeing, close did smyle,
To weet how he her love away did steale,
And bad that none their joyous treason should reveale.

VI
The learned lover lost no time nor tyde,
That least avantage mote to him afford,

Yet bore so faire a sayle, that none espyde
His secret drift, till he her layd abord.
When so in open place and commune bord
He fortun'd her to meet, with commune speach
He courted her, yet bayted every word,
That his ungentle hoste n'ote him appeach
Of vile ungentlenesse, or hospitages breach.

VII
But when apart (if ever her apart)
He found, then his false engins fast he plyde,
And all the sleights unbosomd in his hart;
He sigh'd, he sobd, he swownd, he perdy dyde,
And cast himselfe on ground her fast besyde:
Tho, when againe he him bethought to live,
He wept, and wayld, and false laments belyde,
Saying, but if she mercie would him give,
That he mote algates dye, yet did his death forgive.

VIII
And otherwhyles with amorous delights
And pleasing toyes he would her entertaine,
Now singing sweetly, to surprize her sprights,
Now making layes of love and lovers paine,
Bransles, ballads, vierlayes, and verses vaine;
Oft purposes, oft riddles he devysd,
And thousands like, which flowed in his braine,
With which he fed her fancy, and entysd
To take to his new love, and leave her old despysd.

IX
And every where he might, and everie while,
He did her service dewtifull, and sewd
At hand with humble pride and pleasing guile,
So closely yet, that none but she it vewd,
Who well perceived all, and all indewd.
Thus finely did he his false nets dispred,
With which he many weake harts had subdewd
Of yore, and many had ylike misled:
What wonder then, if she were likewise carried?

X
No fort so fensible, no wals so strong,
But that continuall battery will rive,
Or daily siege, through dispurvayaunce long
And lacke of reskewes, will to parley drive;
And peece, that unto parley eare will give,
Will shortly yield it selfe, and will be made
The vassall of the victors will bylive:
That stratageme had oftentimes assayd
This crafty paramoure, and now it plaine displayd.

XI
For through his traines he her intrapped hath,
That she her love and hart hath wholy sold
To him, without regard of gaine or scath,
Or care of credite, or of husband old,
Whom she hath vow'd to dub a fayre cucquold.
Nought wants but time and place, which shortly shee
Devized hath, and to her lover told.
It pleased well: so well they both agree;
So readie rype to ill, ill wemens counsels bee.

XII
Darke was the evening, fit for lovers stealth,
When chaunst Malbecco busie be elsewhere,
She to his closet went, where all his wealth
Lay hid: thereof she countlesse summes did reare,
The which she meant away with her to beare;
The rest she fyr'd for sport, or for despight;
As Hellene, when she saw aloft appeare
The Trojane flames, and reach to hevens hight,
Did clap her hands, and joyed at that dolefull sight.

XIII
This second Helene, fayre Dame Hellenore,
The whiles her husband ran with sory haste,
To quench the flames which she had tyn'd before,
Laught at his foolish labour spent in waste,
And ran into her lovers armes right fast;
Where streight embraced, she to him did cry
And call alowd for helpe, ere helpe were past,
For lo! that guest did beare her forcibly,
And meant to ravish her, that rather had to dy.

XIV
The wretched man, hearing her call for ayd,
And ready seeing him with her to fly,
In his disquiet mind was much dismayd:
But when againe he backeward cast his eye,
And saw the wicked fire so furiously
Consume his hart, and scorch his idoles face,
He was therewith distressed diversely,
Ne wist he how to turne, nor to what place:
Was never wretched man in such a wofull cace.

XV
Ay when to him she cryde, to her he turnd,
And left the fire; love money overcame:
But when he marked how his money burnd,
He left his wife; money did love disclame:
Both was he loth to loose his loved dame,

And loth to leave his liefest pelfe behinde,
Yet sith he n'ote save both, he sav'd that same
Which was the dearest to his dounghill minde,
The god of his desire, the joy of misers blinde.

XVI
Thus whilest all things in troublous uprore were,
And all men busie to suppresse the flame,
The loving couple neede no reskew feare,
But leasure had and liberty to frame
Their purpost flight, free from all mens reclame;
And Night, the patronesse of love-stealth fayre,
Gave them safeconduct, till to end they came:
So beene they gone yfere, a wanton payre
Of lovers loosely knit, where list them to repayre.

XVII
Soone as the cruell flames yslaked were,
Malbecco, seeing how his losse did lye,
Out of the flames, which he had quencht whylere,
Into huge waves of griefe and gealosye
Full deepe emplonged was, and drowned nye
Twixt inward doole and felonous despight:
He rav'd, he wept, he stampt, he lowd did cry,
And all the passions that in man may light
Did him attonce oppresse, and vex his caytive spright.

XVIII
Long thus he chawd the cud of inward griefe,
And did consume his gall with anguish sore:
Still when he mused on his late mischiefe,
Then still the smart thereof increased more,
And seemd more grievous then it was before:
At last, when sorrow he saw booted nought,
Ne griefe might not his love to him restore,
He gan devise how her he reskew mought;
Ten thousand wayes he cast in his confused thought.

XIX
At last resolving, like a pilgrim pore,
To search her forth, where so she might be fond,
And bearing with him treasure in close store,
The rest he leaves in ground: so takes in hond
To seeke her endlong both by sea and lond.
Long he her sought, he sought her far and nere,
And every where that he mote understond
Of knights and ladies any meetings were,
And of eachone he mett he tidings did inquere.

XX
But all in vaine; his woman was too wise,

Ever to come into his clouch againe,
And hee too simple ever to surprise
The jolly Paridell, for all his paine.
One day, as hee forpassed by the plaine
With weary pace, he far away espide
A couple, seeming well to be his twaine,
Which hoved close under a forest side,
As if they lay in wait, or els them selves did hide.

XXI
Well weened hee that those the same mote bee,
And as he better did their shape avize,
Him seemed more their maner did agree;
For th' one was armed all in warlike wize,
Whom to be Paridell he did devize;
And th' other, al yclad in garments light,
Discolourd like to womanish disguise,
He did resemble to his lady bright,
And ever his faint hart much earned at the sight.

XXII
And ever faine he towards them would goe,
But yet durst not for dread approchen nie,
But stood aloofe, unweeting what to doe,
Till that prickt forth with loves extremity,
That is the father of fowle gealosy,
He closely nearer crept, the truth to weet:
But, as he nigher drew, he easily
Might scerne that it was not his sweetest sweet,
Ne yet her belamour, the partner of his sheet.

XXIII
But it was scornefull Braggadochio,
That with his servant Trompart hoverd there,
Sith late he fled from his too earnest foe:
Whom such whenas Malbecco spyed clere,
He turned backe, and would have fled arere;
Till Trompart ronning hastely, him did stay,
And bad before his soveraine lord appere:
That was him loth, yet durst he not gainesay,
And comming him before, low louted on the lay.

XXIV
The boaster at him sternely bent his browe,
As if he could have kild him with his looke,
That to the ground him meekely made to bowe,
And awfull terror deepe into him strooke,
That every member of his body quooke.
Said he, 'Thou man of nought, what doest thou here,
Unfitly furnisht with thy bag and booke,
Where I expected one with shield and spere,

To prove some deeds of armes upon an equall pere?'

XXV
The wretched man at his imperious speach
Was all abasht, and low prostrating, said:
'Good sir, let not my rudenes be no breach
Unto your patience, ne be ill ypaid;
For I unwares this way by fortune straid,
A silly pilgrim driven to distresse,
That seeke a lady—' There he suddein staid,
And did the rest with grievous sighes suppresse,
While teares stood in his eies, few drops of bitternesse.

XXVI
'What lady, man?' said Trompart. 'Take good hart,
And tell thy griefe, if any hidden lye:
Was never better time to shew thy smart
Then now that noble succor is thee by,
That is the whole worlds commune remedy.'
That chearful word his weak heart much did cheare,
And with vaine hope his spirits faint supply,
That bold he sayd: 'O most redoubted pere,
Vouchsafe with mild regard a wretches cace to heare.'

XXVII
Then sighing sore, 'It is not long,' saide hee,
'Sith I enjoyd the gentlest dame alive;
Of whom a knight, no knight at all perdee,
But shame of all that doe for honor strive,
By treacherous deceipt did me deprive;
Through open outrage he her bore away,
And with fowle force unto his will did drive,
Which al good knights, that armes do bear this day,
Are bownd for to revenge and punish if they may.

XXVIII
'And you, most noble lord, that can and dare
Redresse the wrong of miserable wight,
Cannot employ your most victorious speare
In better quarell then defence of right,
And for a lady gainst a faithlesse knight:
So shall your glory bee advaunced much,
And all faire ladies magnify your might,
And eke my selfe, albee I simple such,
Your worthy paine shall wel reward with guerdon rich.'

XXIX
With that out of his bouget forth he drew
Great store of treasure, therewith him to tempt;
But he on it lookt scornefully askew,
As much disdeigning to be so misdempt,

Or a war-monger to be basely nempt;
And sayd: 'Thy offers base I greatly loth,
And eke thy words uncourteous and unkempt:
I tread in dust thee and thy money both,
That, were it not for shame—' So turned from him wroth.

XXX
But Trompart, that his maistres humor knew,
In lofty looks to hide an humble minde,
Was inly tickled with that golden vew,
And in his eare him rownded close behinde:
Yet stoupt he not, but lay still in the winde,
Waiting advauntage on the pray to sease;
Till Trompart, lowly to the grownd inclinde,
Besought him his great corage to appease,
And pardon simple man, that rash did him displease.

XXXI
Big looking like a doughty doucepere,
At last he thus: 'Thou clod of vilest clay,
I pardon yield, and with thy rudenes beare;
But weete henceforth, that all that golden pray,
And all that els the vaine world vaunten may,
I loath as doung, ne deeme my dew reward:
Fame is my meed, and glory vertues pay:
But minds of mortal men are muchell mard
And mov'd amisse with massy mucks unmeet regard.

XXXII
'And more, I graunt to thy great misery
Gratious respect; thy wife shall backe be sent,
And that vile knight, who ever that he bee,
Which hath thy lady reft, and knighthood shent,
By Sanglamort my sword, whose deadly dent
The blood hath of so many thousands shedd,
I sweare, ere long shall dearly it repent;
Ne he twixt heven and earth shall hide his hedd,
But soone he shalbe fownd, and shortly doen be dedd.'

XXXIII
The foolish man thereat woxe wondrous blith,
As if the word so spoken were halfe donne,
And humbly thanked him a thousand sith,
That had from death to life him newly wonne.
Tho forth the boaster marching, brave begonne
His stolen steed to thunder furiously,
As if he heaven and hell would overonne,
And all the world confound with cruelty,
That much Malbecco joyed in his jollity.

XXXIV

Thus long they three together traveiled,
Through many a wood and many an uncouth way,
To seeke his wife, that was far wandered:
But those two sought nought but the present pray,
To weete, the treasure which he did bewray,
On which their eies and harts were wholly sett,
With purpose how they might it best betray;
For sith the howre that first he did them lett
The same behold, therwith their keene desires were whett.

XXXV
It fortuned, as they together far'd,
They spide, where Paridell came pricking fast
Upon the plaine, the which him selfe prepar'd
To giust with that brave straunger knight a cast,
As on adventure by the way he past:
Alone he rode without his paragone;
For having filcht her bells, her up he cast
To the wide world, and let her fly alone;
He nould be clogd. So had he served many one.

XXXVI
The gentle lady, loose at randon lefte,
The greene-wood long did walke, and wander wide
At wilde adventure, like a forlorne wefte,
Till on a day the Satyres her espide
Straying alone withouten groome or guide:
Her up they tooke, and with them home her ledd,
With them as housewife ever to abide,
To milk their gotes, and make them cheese and bredd,
And every one as commune good her handeled:

XXXVII
That shortly she Malbecco has forgott,
And eke Sir Paridell, all were he deare;
Who from her went to seeke another lott,
And now by fortune was arrived here,
Where those two guilers with Malbecco were.
Soone as the oldman saw Sir Paridell,
He fainted, and was almost dead with feare,
Ne word he had to speake, his griefe to tell,
But to him louted low, and greeted goodly well;

XXXVIII
And after asked him for Hellenore.
'I take no keepe of her,' sayd Paridell,
'She wonneth in the forrest there before.'
So forth he rode, as his adventure fell;
The whiles the boaster from his loftie sell
Faynd to alight, something amisse to mend;
But the fresh swayne would not his leasure dwell,

But went his way; whom when he passed kend,
He up remounted light, and after faind to wend.

XXXIX
'Perdy nay,' said Malbecco, 'shall ye not:
But let him passe as lightly as he came:
For litle good of him is to be got,
And mickle perill to bee put to shame.
But let us goe to seeke my dearest dame,
Whom he hath left in yonder forest wyld:
For of her safety in great doubt I ame,
Least salvage beastes her person have despoyld:
Then all the world is lost, and we in vaine have toyld.'

XL
They all agree, and forward them addrest:
'Ah! but,' said crafty Trompart, 'weete ye well,
That yonder in that wastefull wildernesse
Huge monsters haunt, and many dangers dwell;
Dragons, and minotaures, and feendes of hell,
And many wilde woodmen, which robbe and rend
All traveilers; therefore advise ye well,
Before ye enterprise that way to wend:
One may his journey bring too soone to evill end.'

XLI
Malbecco stopt in great astonishment,
And with pale eyes fast fixed on the rest,
Their counsell crav'd, in daunger imminent.
Said Trompart: 'You, that are the most opprest
With burdein of great treasure, I thinke best
Here for to stay in safetie behynd;
My lord and I will search the wide forest.'
That counsell pleased not Malbeccoes mynd;
For he was much afraid, him selfe alone to fynd.

XLII
'Then is it best,' said he, 'that ye doe leave
Your treasure here in some security,
Either fast closed in some hollow greave,
Or buried in the ground from jeopardy,
Till we returne againe in safety:
As for us two, least doubt of us ye have,
Hence farre away we will blyndfolded ly,
Ne privy bee unto your treasures grave.'
It pleased: so he did. Then they march forward brave.

XLIII
Now when amid the thickest woodes they were,
They heard a noyse of many bagpipes shrill,
And shrieking hububs them approching nere,

Which all the forest did with horrour fill:
That dreadfull sound the bosters hart did thrill
With such amazment, that in hast he fledd,
Ne ever looked back for good or ill,
And after him eke fearefull Trompart spedd;
The old man could not fly, but fell to ground half dedd.

XLIV
Yet afterwardes close creeping as he might,
He in a bush did hyde his fearefull hedd.
The jolly Satyres, full of fresh delight,
Came dauncing forth, and with them nimbly ledd
Faire Helenore, with girlonds all bespredd,
Whom their May-lady they had newly made:
She, proude of that new honour which they redd,
And of their lovely fellowship full glade,
Daunst lively, and her face did with a lawrell shade.

XLV
The silly man that in the thickeet lay
Saw all this goodly sport, and grieved sore,
Yet durst he not against it doe or say,
But did his hart with bitter thoughts engore,
To see th' unkindnes of his Hellenore.
All day they daunced with great lustyhedd,
And with their horned feet the greene gras wore,
The whiles their gotes upon the brouzes fedd,
Till drouping Phœbus gan to hyde his golden hedd.

XLVI
Tho up they gan their mery pypes to trusse,
And all their goodly heardes did gather rownd,
But every Satyre first did give a busse
To Hellenore: so busses did abound.
Now gan the humid vapour shed the grownd
With perly deaw, and th' earthes gloomy shade
Did dim the brightnesse of the welkin rownd,
That every bird and beast awarned made
To shrowd themselves, whiles sleepe their sences did invade.

XLVII
Which when Malbecco saw, out of his bush
Upon his hands and feete he crept full light,
And like a gote emongst the gotes did rush,
That through the helpe of his faire hornes on hight,
And misty dampe of misconceyving night,
And eke through likenesse of his gotish beard,
He did the better counterfeite aright:
So home he marcht emongst the horned heard.
That none of all the Satyres him espyde or heard.

XLVIII
At night, when all they went to sleepe, he vewd
Whereas his lovely wife emongst them lay,
Embraced of a Satyre rough and rude,
Who all the night did minde his joyous play:
Nine times he heard him come aloft ere day,
That all his hart with gealosy did swell;
But yet that nights ensample did swell;
That not for nought his wife them loved so well,
When one so oft a night did ring his matins bell.

XLIX
So closely as he could, he to them crept,
When wearie of their sport to sleepe they fell,
And to his wife, that now full soundly slept,
He whispered in her eare, and did her tell,
That it was he, which by her side did dwell,
And therefore prayd her wake, to heare him plaine.
As one out of a dreame not waked well,
She turnd her, and returned backe againe:
Yet her for to awake he did the more constraine.

L
At last with irkesom trouble she abrayd;
And then perceiving, that it was indeed
Her old Malbecco, which did her upbrayd
With loosenesse of her love and loathly deed,
She was astonisht with exceeding dreed,
And would have wakt the Satyre by her syde;
But he her prayd, for mercy or for meed,
To save his life, ne let him be descryde,
But hearken to his lore, and all his counsell hyde.

LI
Tho gan he her perswade to leave that lewd
And loathsom life, of God and man abhord,
And home returne, where all should be renewd
With prefect peace and bandes of fresh accord,
And she received againe to bed and bord,
As if no trespas ever had beene donne:
But she it all refused at one word,
And by no meanes would to his will be wonne,
But chose emongst the jolly Satyres still to wonne.

LII
He wooed her till day spring he espyde;
But all in vaine: and then turnd to the heard,
Who butted him with hornes on every syde,
And trode downe in the durst, where his hore beard
Was fowly dight, and he of death afeard.
Early, before the heavens fairest light

Out of the ruddy east was fully reard,
The heardes out of their foldes were loosed quight,
And he emongst the rest crept forth in sory plight.

LIII
So soone as he the prison dore did pas,
He ran as fast as both his feet could beare,
And never looked who behind him was,
Ne scarsely who before: like as a beare,
That creeping close, amongst the hives to reare
An hony combe, the wakefull full dogs espy,
And him assayling, sore his carkas teare,
That hardly he with life away does fly,
Ne stayes, till safe him selfe he see from jeopardy.

LIV
Ne stayd he, till he came unto the place,
Where late his treasure he entombed had;
Where when he found it not (for Trompart bace
Had it purloyned for his maister bad)
With extreme fury he became quite mad,
And ran away, ran with him selfe away:
That who so straungely had him seene bestadd,
With upstart haire and staring eyes dismay,
From Limbo lake him late escaped sure would say.

LV
High over hilles and over dales he fledd,
As if the wind him on his winges had borne,
Ne bancke nor bush could stay him, when he spedd
His nimble feet, as treading still on thorne:
Griefe, and despight, and gealosy, and scorne
Did all the way him follow hard behynd,
And he himselfe himselfe loath'd so forlorne,
So shamefully forlorne of womankynd;
That, as a snake, still lurked in his wounded mynd.

LVI
Still fled he forward, looking backward still,
Ne stayd his flight, nor fearefull agony,
Till that he came unto a rocky hill,
Over the sea suspended dreadfully,
That living creature it would terrify
To looke adowne, or upward to the hight:
Form thence he threw him selfe dispiteously,
All desperate of his fore-dammed spright,
That seemd no help for him was left in living sight.

LVII
But through long anguish and selfe-murdring thought,
He was so wasted and forpined quight,

That all his substance was consum'd to nought,
And nothing left, but like an aery spright,
That on the rockes he fell so flit and light,
That he thereby receiv'd no hurt at all;
But chaunced on a craggy cliff to light;
Whence he with crooked clawes so long did crall,
That at the last he found a cave with entrance small.

LVIII
Into the same he creepes, and thenceforth there
Resolv'd to build his balefull mansion,
In drery darkenes, and continuall feare
Of that rocks fall, which ever and anon
Threates with huge ruine him to fall upon,
That he dare never sleepe, but that one eye
Still ope he keepes for that occasion;
Ne ever rests he in tranquillity,
The roring billowes beat his bowre so boystrously.

LIX
Ne ever is he wont on ought to feed
But todes and frogs, his pasture poysonous,
Which in his cold complexion doe breed
A filthy blood, or humour rancorous,
Matter of doubt and dread suspitious,
That doth with curelesse care consume the hart,
Corrupts the stomacke with gall vitious,
Croscuts the liver with internall smart,
And doth transfixe the soule with deathes eternall dart.

LX
Yet can he never dye, but dying lives,
And doth himselfe with sorrow new sustaine,
That death and life attonce unto him gives,
And painefull pleasure turnes to pleasing paine.
There dwels he ever, miserable swaine,
Hatefull both to him selfe and every wight;
Where he, through privy griefe and horrour vaine,
Is woxen so deform'd, that he has quight
Forgot he was a man, and Gelosy is hight.

CANTO XI

Britomart chaceth Ollyphant;
Findes Scudamour distrest:
Assayes the house of Busyrane,
Where Loves spoyles are exprest.

I
O hatefull hellish snake! what Furie furst
Brought thee from balefull house of Proserpine,
Where in her bosome she thee long had nurst,
And fostred up with bitter milke of tine,
Fowle Gealosy! that turnest love divine
To joylesse dread, and mak'st the loving hart
With hatefull thoughts to languish and to pine,
And feed it selfe with selfe-consuming smart?
Of all the passions in the mind thou vilest art.

II
O let him far be banished away,
And in his stead let Love for ever dwell,
Sweete Love, that doth his golden wings embay
In blessed nectar, and pure pleasures well,
Untroubled of vile feare or bitter fell.
And ye, faire ladies, that your kingdomes make
In th' harts of men, them governe wisely well,
And of faire Britomart ensample take,
That was as trew in love as turtle to her make.

III
Who with Sir Satyrane, as earst ye red,
Forth ryding from Malbeccoes hostlesse hous,
Far off aspyde a young man, the which fled
From an huge geaunt, that with hideous
And hatefull outrage long him chaced thus;
It was that Ollyphant, the brother deare
Of that Argante vile and vitious,
From whom the Squyre of Dames was reft whylere;
This all as bad as she, and worse, if worse ought were.

IV
For as the sister did in feminine
And filthy lust exceede all woman kinde,
So he surpassed his sex masculine,
In beastly use, all that I ever finde:
Whom when as Britomart beheld behinde
The fearefull boy so greedily poursew,
She was emmoved in her noble minde
T' employ her puissaunce to his reskew,
And pricked fiercely forward, where she did him vew.

V
Ne was Sir Satyrane her far behinde,
But with like fiercenesse did ensew the chace:
Whom when the gyaunt saw, he soone resinde
His former suit, and from them fled apace:
They after both, and boldly bad him bace,

And each did strive the other to outgoe;
But he them both outran a wondrous space,
For he was long, and swift as any roe,
And now made better speed, t' escape his feared foe.

VI
It was not Satyrane, whom he did feare,
But Britomart the flowre of chastity;
For he the powre of chaste hands might not beare,
But alwayes did their dread encounter fly:
And now so fast his feet he did apply,
That he has gotten to a forrest neare,
Where he is shrowded in security.
The wood they enter, and search everie where;
They searched diversely, so both divided were.

VII
Fayre Britomart so long him followed,
That she at last came to a fountaine sheare,
By which there lay a knight all wallowed
Upon the grassy ground, and by him neare
His haberjeon, his helmet, and his speare:
A little of, his shield was rudely throwne,
On which the Winged Boy in colours cleare
Depeincted was, full easie to be knowne,
And he thereby, where ever it in field was showne.

VIII
His face upon the grownd did groveling ly,
As if he had beene slombring in the shade,
That the brave mayd would not for courtesy
Out of his quiet slomber him abrade,
Nor seeme too suddeinly him to invade:
Still as she stood, she heard with grievous throb
Him grone, as if his hart were peeces made,
And with most painefull pangs to sigh and sob,
That pitty did the virgins hart of patience rob.

IX
At last forth breaking into bitter plaintes
He sayd: 'O soverayne Lord, that sit'st on hye,
And raignst in blis emongst thy blessed saintes,
How suffrest thou such shamefull cruelty,
So long unwreaked of thine enimy?
Or hast thou, Lord, of good mens cause no heed?
Or doth thy justice sleepe, and silently?
What booteth then the good and righteous deed,
If goodnesse find no grace, nor righteousnes no meed?

X
'If good find grace, and righteousnes reward,

Why then is Amoret in caytive band,
Sith that more bounteous creature never far'd
On foot upon the face of living land?
Or if that hevenly justice may withstand
The wrongfull outrage of unrighteous men,
Why then is Busirane with wicked hand
Suffred, these seven monethes day in secret den
My lady and my love so cruelly to pen?

XI
'My lady and my love is cruelly pend
In dolefull darkenes from the vew of day,
Whilest deadly torments doe her chast brest rend,
And the sharpe steele doth rive her hart in tway,
All for she Scudamore will not denay.
Yet thou, vile man, vile Scudamore, art sound,
Ne canst her ayde, ne canst her foe dismay;
Unworthy wretch to tread upon the ground,
For whom so faire a lady feeles so sore a wound.'

XII
There an huge heape of singulfes did oppresse
His strugling soule, and swelling throbs empeach
His foltring toung with pangs of drerinesse,
Choking the remnant of his plaintife speach,
As if his dayes were come to their last reach.
Which when she heard, and saw the ghastly fit,
Threatning into his life to make a breach,
Both with great ruth and terrour she was smit,
Fearing least from her cage the wearie soule would flit.

XIII
Tho stouping downe, she him amoved light;
Who, therewith somewhat starting, up gan looke,
And seeing him behind a stranger knight,
Whereas no living creature he mistooke,
With great indignaunce he that sight forsooke,
And downe againe himselfe disdainefully
Abjecting, th' earth with his faire forhead strooke:
Which the bold virgin seeing, gan apply
Fit medcine to his griefe, and spake thus courtesly:

XIV
'Ah! gentle knight, whose deepe conceived griefe
Well seemes t' exceede the powre of patience,
Yet if that hevenly grace some good reliefe
You send, submit you to High Providence,
And ever in your noble hart prepense,
That all the sorrow in the world is lesse
Then vertues might and values confidence.
For who nill bide the burden of distresse

Must not here thinke to live: for life is wretchednesse.

XV
'Therefore, faire sir, doe comfort to you take,
And freely read what wicked felon so
Hath outrag'd you, and thrald your gentle make.
Perhaps this hand may helpe to ease your woe,
And wreake your sorrow on your cruell foe;
At least it faire endevour will apply.'
Those feeling words so neare the quicke did goe,
That up his head he reared easily,
And leaning on his elbowe, these few words lett fly:

XVI
'What boots it plaine that cannot be redrest,
And sow vaine sorrow in a fruitlesse eare,
Sith powre of hand, nor skill of learned brest,
Ne worldly price cannot redeeme my deare
Out of her thraldome and continuall feare?
For he, the tyrant, which her hath in ward
By strong enchauntments and blacke magicke leare,
Hath in a dungeon deepe her close embard,
And many dreadfull feends hath pointed to her gard.

XVII
'There he tormenteth her most terribly,
And day and night afflicts with mortall paine,
Because to yield him love she doth deny,
Once to me yold, not to be yolde againe:
But yet by torture he would her constraine
Love to conceive in her disdainfull brest;
Till so she doe, she must in doole remaine,
Ne may by living meanes be thence relest:
What boots it then to plaine that cannot be redrest?'

XVIII
With this sad hersall of his heavy stresse
The warlike damzell was empassiond sore,
And sayd: 'Sir knight, your cause is nothing lesse
Then is your sorrow, certes, if not more;
For nothing so much pitty doth implore,
As gentle ladyes helplesse misery.
But yet, if please ye listen to my lore,
I will, with proofe of last extremity,
Deliver her fro thence, or with her for you dy.'

XIX
'Ah! gentlest knight alive,' sayd Scudamore,
'What huge heroicke magnanimity
Dwells in thy bounteous brest? what couldst thou more,
If shee were thine, and thou as now am I?

O spare thy happy daies, and them apply
To better boot, but let me die, that ought;
More is more losse: one is enough to dy.'
'Life is not lost,' said she, 'for which is bought
Endlesse renowm, that more then death is to be sought.'

XX
Thus shee at length persuaded him to rise,
And with her wend, to see what new successe
Mote him befall upon new enterprise:
His armes, which he had vowed to disprofesse,
She gathered up and did about him dresse,
And his forwandred steed unto him gott:
So forth they both yfere make their progresse,
And march not past the mountenaunce of a shott,
Till they arriv'd whereas their purpose they did plott.

XXI
There they dismounting, drew their weapons bold,
And stoutly came unto the castle gate,
Whereas no gate they found, them to withhold,
Nor ward to wait at morne and evening late;
But in the porch, that did them sore amate,
A flaming fire, ymixt with smouldry smoke
And stinking sulphure, that with griesly hate
And dreadfull horror did all entraunce choke,
Enforced them their forward footing to revoke.

XXII
Greatly thereat was Britomart dismayd,
Ne in that stownd wist how her selfe to beare;
For daunger vaine it were to have assayd
That cruell element, which all things feare,
Ne none can suffer to approchen neare:
And turning backe to Scudamour, thus sayd:
'What monstrous enmity provoke we heare,
Foolhardy as th' Earthes children, the which made
Batteill against the gods? so we a god invade.

XXIII
'Daunger without discretion to attempt
Inglorious and beastlike is: therefore, sir knight,
Aread what course of you is safest dempt,
And how we with our foe may come to fight.'
'This is,' quoth he, 'the dolorous despight,
Which earst to you I playnd: for neither may
This fire be quencht by any witt or might,
Ne yet by any meanes remov'd away;
So mighty be th' enchauntments which the same do stay.

XXIV

'What is there ells, but cease these fruitlesse paines,
And leave me to my former languishing?
Faire Amorett must dwell in wicked chaines,
And Scudamore here die with sorrowing.'
'Perdy, not so,' saide shee; 'for shameful thing
Yt were t' abandon noble chevisaunce,
For shewe of perill, without venturing:
Rather let try extremities of chaunce,
Then enterprised praise for dread to disavaunce.'

XXV
Therewith, resolv'd to prove her utmost might,
Her ample shield she threw before her face,
And her swords point directing forward right,
Assayld the flame, the which eftesoones gave place,
And did it selfe divide with equall space,
That through she passed, as a thonder bolt
Perceth the yielding ayre, and doth displace
The soring clouds into sad showres ymolt;
So to her yold the flames, and did their force revolt.

XXVI
Whome whenas Scudamour saw past the fire,
Safe and untoucht, he likewise gan assay,
With greedy will and envious desire,
And bad the stubborne flames to yield him way:
But cruell Mulciber would not obay
His threatfull pride, but did the more augment
His mighty rage, and with imperious sway
Him forst (maulgre) his fercenes to relent,
And backe retire, all scorcht and pitifully brent.

XXVII
With huge impatience he inly swelt,
More for great sorrow that he could not pas
Then for the burning torment which he felt;
That with fell woodnes he effierced was,
And wilfully him throwing on the gras,
Did beat and bounse his head and brest ful sore;
The whiles the championesse now entred has
The utmost rowme, and past the formost dore,
The utmost rowme, abounding with all precious store.

XXVIII
For round about, the walls yclothed were
With goodly arras of great majesty,
Woven with gold and silke so close and nere,
That the rich metall lurked privily,
As faining to be hidd from envious eye;
Yet here, and there, and every where unwares
It shewd it selfe, and shone unwillingly;

Like a discolourd snake, whose hidden snares
Through the greene gras his long bright burnisht back declares.

XXIX
And in those tapets weren fashioned
Many faire pourtraicts, and many a faire feate;
And all of love, and al of lusty-hed,
As seemed by their semblaunt, did entreat;
And eke all Cupids warres they did repeate,
And cruell battailes, which he whilome fought
Gainst all the gods, to make his empire great;
Besides the huge massacres, which he wrought
On mighty kings and kesars, into thraldome brought.

XXX
Therein was writt, how often thondring Jove
Had felt the point of his hart percing dart,
And leaving heavens kingdome, here did rove
In straunge disguize, to slake his scalding smart;
Now like a ram, faire Helle to pervart,
Now like a bull, Europa to withdraw:
Ah! how the fearefull ladies tender hart
Did lively seeme to tremble, when she saw
The huge seas under her t' obay her servaunts law!

XXXI
Soone after that, into a golden showre
Him selfe he chaung'd, faire Danaë to vew,
And through the roofe of her strong brasen towre
Did raine into her lap an hony dew,
The whiles her foolish garde, that litle knew
Of such deceipt, kept th' yron dore fast bard,
And watcht, that none should enter nor issew;
Vaine was the watch, and bootlesse all the ward,
Whenas the god to golden hew him selfe transfard.

XXXII
Then was he turnd into a snowy swan,
To win faire Leda to his lovely trade:
O wondrous skill and sweet wit of the man,
That her in daffadillies sleeping made,
From scorching heat her daintie limbes to shade:
Whiles the proud bird, ruffing his fethers wyde
And brushing his faire brest, did her invade!
Shee slept, yet twixt her eielids closely spyde
How towards her he rusht, and smiled at his pryde.

XXXIII
Then shewd it how the Thebane Semelee,
Deceivd of gealous Juno, did require
To see him in his soverayne majestee,

Armd with his thunderbolts and lightning fire,
Whens dearely she with death bought her desire.
But faire Alcmena better match did make,
Joying his love in likenes more entire:
Three nights in one they say that for her sake
He then did put, her pleasures lenger to partake.

XXXIV

Twise was he seene in soaring eagles shape,
And with wide winges to beat the buxome ayre:
Once, when he with Asterie did scape,
Againe, when as the Trojane boy so fayre
He snatcht from Ida hill, and with him bare:
Wondrous delight it was, there to behould
How the rude shepheards after him did stare,
Trembling through feare least down he fallen should,
And often to him calling to take surer hould.

XXXV

In Satyres shape Antiopa he snatcht:
And like a fire, when he Aegin' assayd:
A shepeheard, when Mnemosyne he catcht:
And like a serpent to the Thracian mayd.
Whyles thus on earth great Jove these pageaunts playd,
The Winged Boy did thrust into his throne,
And scoffing, thus unto his mother sayd:
'Lo! now the hevens obey to me alone,
And take me for their Jove, whiles Jove to earth is gone.'

XXXVI

And thou, faire Phœbus, in thy colours bright
Wast there enwoven, and the sad distresse
In which that boy thee plonged, for despight
That thou bewray'dst his mothers wantonnesse,
When she with Mars was meynt in joyfulnesse:
Forthy he thrild thee with a leaden dart,
To love faire Daphne, which thee loved lesse:
Lesse she thee lov'd then was thy just desart,
Yet was thy love her death, and her death was thy smart.

XXXVII

So lovedst thou the lusty Hyacinct,
So lovedst thou the faire Coronis deare:
Yet both are of thy haplesse hand extinct,
Yet both in flowres doe live, and love thee beare,
The one a paunce, the other a sweet breare:
For griefe whereof, ye mote have lively seene
The god himselfe rending his golden heare,
And breaking quite his garlond ever greene,
With other signes of sorrow and impatient teene.

XXXVIII
Both for those two, and for his owne deare sonne,
The sonne of Climene, he did repent,
Who, bold to guide the charet of the sunne,
Himselfe in thousand peeces fondly rent,
And all the world with flashing fire brent:
So like, that all the walles did seeme to flame.
Yet cruell Cupid, not herewith content,
Forst him eftsoones to follow other game,
And love a shephards daughter for his dearest dame.

XXXIX
He loved Isse for his dearest dame,
And for her sake her cattell fedd a while,
And for her sake a cowheard vile became,
The servant of Admetus, cowheard vile,
Whiles that from heaven he suffered exile.
Long were to tell each other lovely fitt,
Now like a lyon, hunting after spoile,
Now like a stag, now like a faulcon flit:
All which in that faire arras was most lively writ.

XL
Next unto him was Neptune pictured,
In his divine resemblance wondrous lyke:
His face was rugged, and his hoarie hed
Dropped with brackish deaw; his threeforkt pyke
He stearnly shooke, and therewith fierce did stryke
The raging billowes, that on every syde
They trembling stood, and made a long broad dyke,
That his swift charet might have passage wyde,
Which foure great hippodames did draw in temewise tyde.

XLI
His seahorsed did seeme to snort amayne,
And from their nosethrilles blow the brynie streame,
That made the sparckling waves to smoke agayne,
And flame with gold, but the white fomy creame
Did shine with silver, and shoot forth his beame.
The god himselfe did pensive seeme and sad,
And hond adowne his head, as he did dreame:
For privy love his brest empierced had,
Ne ought but deare Bisaltis ay could make him glad.

XLII
He loved eke Iphimedia deare,
And Aeolus faire daughter, Arne hight,
For whom he turnd him selfe into a steare,
And fedd on fodder, to beguile her sight.
Also to win Deucalions daughter bright,
He turnd him selfe into a dolphin fayre;

And like a winged horse he tooke his flight,
To snaky-locke Medusa to repayre,
On whom he got faire Pegasus, that flitteth in the arye.

XLIII
Next Saturne was, (but who would ever weene
That sullein Saturne ever weend to love?
Yet love is sullein, and Saturnlike seene,
As he did for Erigone it prove,)
That to a centaure did him selfe transmove.
So proov'd it eke that gratious good of wine,
When, for to compasse Philliras hard love,
He turnd himselfe into a fruitfull vine,
And into her faire bosome made his grapes decline.

XLIV
Long were to tell the amorous assayes,
And gentle pangues, with which he maked meeke
The mightie Mars, to learne his wanton playes:
How oft for Venus, and how often eek
For many other nymphes he sore did shreek,
With womanish teares, and with unwarlike smarts,
Privily moystening his horrid cheeke.
There was he painted full of burning dartes,
And many wide woundes launched through his inner partes.

XLV
Ne did he spare (so cruell was the elfe)
His owne deare mother, (ah! why should he so?)
Ne did he spare sometime to pricke himselfe,
That he might taste the sweet consuming woe,
Which he had wrought to many others moe.
But to declare the mournfull tragedyes,
And spoiles, wherewith he all the ground did strow,
More eath to number with how many eyes
High heven beholdes sad lovers nightly theeveryes.

XLVI
Kings, queenes, lords, ladies, knights, and damsels gent
Were heap'd together with the vulgar sort,
And mingled with the raskall rablement,
Without respect of person or of port,
To shew Dan Cupids powre and great effort:
And round about, a border was entrayld
Of broken bowes and arrowes shivered short,
And a long bloody river through them rayld,
So lively and so like that living sence it fayld.

XLVII
And at the upper end of that faire rowme,
There was an altar built of pretious stone,

Of passing valew and of great renowme,
On which there stood an image all alone
Of massy gold, which with his owne light shone;
And winges it had with sondry colours dight,
More sondry colours then the pround pavone
Beares in his boasted fan, or Iris bright,
When her discolourd bow she spreds through hevens hight.

XLVIII
Blyndfold he was, and in his cruell fist
A mortall bow and arrowes Keene did hold,
With which he shot at randon, when him list,
Some headed with sad lead, some with pure gold;
(Ah! man, beware how thou those dartes behold.)
A wounded dragon under him did ly,
Whose hideous tayle his lefte foot did enfold,
And with a shaft was shot through either eye,
That no man forth might draw, ne no man remedye.

XLIX
And underneath his feet was written thus,
Unto the victor of the gods this bee:
And all the people in that ample hous
Did to that image bowe their humble knee,
And oft committed fowle idolatree.
That wondrous sight faire Britomart amazd,
Ne seeing could her wonder satisfie,
But ever more and more upon it gazd,
The whiles the passing brightnes her fraile sences dazd.

L
Tho as she backward cast her busie eye,
To search each secrete of that goodly sted,
Over the dore thus written she did spye,
Bee bold: she oft and oft it over-red,
Yet could not find what sence it figured:
But what so were therein or writ or ment,
She was no whit thereby discouraged
From prosecuting of her first intent,
But forward with bold steps into the next roome went.

LI
Much fayrer then the former was that roome,
And richlier by many partes arayd;
For not with arras made in painefull loome,
But with pure gold, it all was overlayd,
Wrought with wilde antickes, which their follies playd
In the rich metall, as they living were:
A thousand monstrous formes therein were made,
Such as false Love doth oft upon him weare,
For Love in thousand monstrous formes doth oft appeare.

LII
And all about, the glistring walles were hong
With warlike spoiles and with victorious prayes
Of mightie conquerours and captaines strong,
Which were whilome captived in their dayes
To cruell Love, and wrought their owne decayes:
Their swerds and speres were broke, and hauberques rent,
And their proud girlonds of tryumphant bayes
Troden in dust with fury insolent,
To shew the victors might and mercilesse intent.

LIII
The warlike mayd, beholding earnestly
The goodly ordinaunce of this rich place,
Did greatly wonder, ne could satisfy
Her greedy eyes with gazing a long space;
But more she mervaild that no footings trace
Nor wight appear'd, but wastefull emptinesse
And solemne silence over all that place:
Straunge thing it seem'd, that none was to possesse
So rich purveyaunce, ne them keepe with carefulnesse.

LIV
And as she lookt about, she did behold
How over that same dore was like wise writ,
Be bolde, be bolde, and every where Be bold,
That much she muz'd, yet could not construe it
By any ridling skill or commune wit.
At last she spyde at that rowmes upper end
Another yron dore, on which was writ,
Be not too bold; whereto though she did bend
Her earnest minde, yet wist not what it might Intend.

LV
Thus she there wayted untill eventyde,
Yet living creature none she saw appeare:
And now sad shadowes gan the world to hyde
From mortall vew, and wrap in darkenes dreare;
Yet nould she d'off her weary armes, for feare
Of secret daunger, ne let sleepe oppresse
Her heavy eyes with natures burdein deare,
But drew her selfe aside in sickernesse,
And her welpointed wepons did about her dresse.

CANTO XII

The maske of Cupid, and th' enchanted

chamber are displayd,
Whence Britomart redeemes faire
Amoret through charmes decayd.

I
Tho, when as chearelesse night ycovered had
Fayre heaven with an universall clowd,
That every wight, dismayd with darkeness sad,
In silence and in sleepe themselves did shrowd,
She heard a shrilling trompet sound alowd,
Signe of nigh battaill, or got victory:
Nought therewith daunted was her courage prowd,
But rather stird to cruell enmity,
Expecting ever when some foe she might descry.

II
With that, an hideous storme of winde arose,
With dreadfull thunder and lightning atwixt,
And an earthquake, as if it streight would lose
The worlds foundations from his centre fixt:
A direfull stench of smoke and sulphure mixt
Ensewd, whose noyunce fild the fearefull sted,
From the fourth howre of night untill the sixt;
Yet the bold Britonesse was nought ydred,
Though much emmov'd, but stedfast still persevered.

III
All suddeinly a stormy whirlwind blew
Throughout the house, that clapped every dore,
With which that yron wicket open flew,
As it with mighty levers had bene tore;
And forth yssewd, as on the readie flore
Of some theatre, a grave personage,
That in his hand a braunch of laurell bore,
With comely haveour and count'nance sage,
Yclad in costly garments, fit for tragicke stage.

IV
Proceeding to the midst, he stil did stand,
As if in minde he somewhat had to say,
And to the vulgare beckning with his hand,
In signe of silence, as to heare a play,
By lively actions he gan bewray
Some argument of matter passioned;
Which doen, he backe retyred soft away,
And passing by, his name discovered,
Ease, on his robe in golden letters cyphered.

V
The noble mayd, still standing, all this vewd,

And merveild at his straunge intendiment:
With that a joyous fellowship issewd
Of minstrales, making goodly meriment,
With wanton bardes, and rymers impudent,
All which together song full chearefully
A lay of loves delight, with sweet concent:
After whom marcht a jolly company,
In manner of a maske, enranged orderly.

VI
The whiles a most delitious harmony
In full straunge notes was sweetly heard to sound,
That the rare sweetnesse of the melody
The feeble sences wholy did confound,
And the frayle soule in deepe delight nigh drownd:
And when it ceast, shrill trompets lowd did bray,
That their report did far away rebound,
And when they ceast, if gan againe to play,
The whiles the maskers marched forth in trim aray.

VII
The first was Fansy, like a lovely boy,
Of rare aspect and beautie without peare,
Matchable ether to that ympe of Troy,
Whom Jove did love and chose his cup to beare,
Or that same daintie lad, which was so deare
To great Alcides, that, when as he dyde,
He wailed womanlike with many a teare,
And every wood and every valley wyde
He fild with Hylas name; the nymphes eke Hylas cryde.

VIII
His garment nether was of silke nor say,
But paynted plumes, in goodly order dight,
Like as the sunburnt Indians do aray
Their tawney bodies, in their proudest plight:
As those same plumes, so seemd he vaine and light,
That by his gate might easily appeare;
For still he far'd as dauncing in delight,
And in his hand a windy fan did beare,
That in the ydle ayre he mov'd still here and theare.

IX
And him beside marcht amorous Desyre,
Who seemd of ryper yeares then th' other swayne,
Yet was that other swayne this elders syre,
And gave him being, commune to them twayne:
His garment was disguysed very vayne,
And his embrodered bonet sat awry;
Twixt both his hands few sparks he close did strayne,
Which still he blew, and kindled busily,

That soone they life conceiv'd, and forth in flames did fly.

X
Next after him went Doubt, who was yclad
In a discolour'd cote of straunge disguyse,
That at his backe a brode capuccio had,
And sleeves dependaunt Albanese-wyse:
He lookt askew with his mistrustfull eyes,
And nycely trode, as thornes lay in his way,
Or that the flore to shrinke he did avyse,
And on a broken reed he still did stay
His feeble steps, which shrunck when hard thereon he lay.

XI
With him went Daunger, cloth'd in ragged weed,
Made of beares skin, that him more dreadfull made,
Yet his owne face was dreadfull, ne did need
Straunge horrour to deforme his griesly shade:
A net in th' one hand, and a rusty blade
In th' other was, this Mischiefe, that Mishap;
With th' one his foes he threatned to invade,
With th' other he his friends ment to enwrap:
For whom he could not kill he practizd to entrap.

XII
Next him was Feare, all arm'd from top to toe,
Yet thought himselfe not safe enough thereby,
But feard each shadow moving too or froe,
And his owne armes when glittering he did spy,
Or clashing heard, he fast away did fly,
As ashes pale of hew, and wingyheeld;
And evermore on Daunger fixt his eye,
Gainst whom he alwayes bent a brasen shield,
Which his right hand unarmed fearefully did wield.

XIII
With him went Hope in rancke, a handsome mayd,
Of chearefull looke and lovely to behold;
In silken samite she was light arayd,
And her fayre lockes were woven up in gold;
She alway smyld, and in her hand did hold
An holy water sprinckle, dipt in deowe,
With which she sprinckled facours mainfold
On whom she list, and did great liking sheowe,
Great liking unto many, but true love of feowe.

XIV
And after them Dissemblaunce and Suspect
Marcht in one rancke, yet an unequall paire:
For she was gentle and of milde aspect,
Courteous to all and seeming debonaire,

Goodly adorned and exceeding faire:
Yet was that all but paynted and pourloynd,
And her bright browes were deckt with borrowed haire:
Her deeds were forged, and her words false coynd,
And alwaies in her hand two clewes of silke she twynd.

XV
But he was fowle, ill favoured, and grim,
Under his eiebrowes looking still askaunce;
And ever as Dissemblaunce laught on him,
He lowrd on her with daungerous eyeglaunce,
Shewing his nature in his countenaunce;
His rolling eies did never rest in place,
But walkte each where, for feare of hid mischaunce;
Holding a lattis still before his face,
Through which he stil did peep, as forward he did pace.

XVI
Next him went Griefe and Fury matcht yfere;
Griefe all in sable sorrowfully clad,
Downe hanging his dull head, with heavy chere,
Yet inly being more then seeming sad:
A paire of pincers in his hand he had,
With which he pincers people to the hart,
That from thenceforth a wretched life they ladd,
In wilfull langnor and consuming smart,
Dying each day with inward wounds of dolours dart.

XVII
But Fury was full ill appareiled
In rags, that naked nigh she did appeare,
With ghastly looks and dreadfull drerihed;
For from her backe her garments she did teare,
And from her head ofte rent her snarled heare:
In her right hand a firebrand shee did tosse
About her head, still roming here and there;
As a dismayed deare in chace embost,
Forgetfull of his safety, hath his right way lost.

XVIII
After them went Displeasure and Pleasaunce,
He looking lompish and full sullein sad,
And hanging downe his heavy countenaunce;
She chearfull fresh and full of joyaunce glad,
As if no sorrow she ne felt ne drad;
That evill matched paire they seemd to bee:
An angry waspe th' one in a viall had,
Th' other in hers an hony-laden bee.
Thus marched these six couples forth in faire degree.

XIX

After all these there marcht a most faire dame,
Led of two grysie villeins, th' one Despight,
The other cleped Cruelty by name:
She, dolefull lady, like a dreary spright
Cald by strong charmes out of eternall night,
Had deathes owne ymage figurd in her face,
Full of sad signes, fearfull to living sight,
Yet in that horror shewd a seemely grace,
And with her feeble feete did move a comely pace.

XX
Her brest all naked, as nett yvory,
Without adorne of gold or silver bright,
Wherewith the craftesman wonts it beautify,
Of her dew honour was despoyled quight,
And a wide wound therein (O ruefull sight!)
Entrenched deep with knyfe accursed keene,
Yet freshly bleeding forth her fainting spright,
(The worke of cruell hand) was to be seene,
That dyde in sanguine red her skin all snowy cleene.

XXI
At that wide orifice her trembling hart
Was drawne forth, and in silver basin layd,
Quite through transfixed with a deadly dart,
And in her blood yet steeming fresh embayd:
And those two villeins, which her steps upstayd,
When her weake feete could scarcely her sustaine,
And fading vitall powers gan to fade,
Her forward still with torture did constraine,
And evermore encreased her consuming paine.

XXII
Next after her, the Winged God him selfe
Came riding on a lion ravenous,
Taught to obay the menage of that elfe,
That man and beast with powre imperious
Subdeweth to his kingdome tyrannous:
His blindfold eies he bad a while unbinde,
That his proud spoile of that same dolorous
Faire dame he might behold in perfect kinde,
Which seene, he much rejoyced in his cruell minde.

XXIII
Of which ful prowd, him selfe up rearing hye,
He looked round about with sterne disdayne,
And did survay his goodly company:
And marshalling the evill ordered traync,
With that the darts which his right hand did straine
Full dreadfully he shooke, that all did quake,
And clapt on hye his coulourd winges twaine,

That all his many it affraide did make:
Tho, blinding him againe, his way he forth did take.

XXIV
Behind him was Reproch, Repentaunce, Shame;
Reproch the first, Shame next, Repent behinde:
Repentaunce feeble, sorowfull, and lame;
Reproch despightful, carelesse, and unkinde;
Shame most ill favour, bestiall, and blinde:
Shame lowrd, Repentaunce sigh'd, Reproch did scould;
Reproch sharpe stings, Repentaunce whips entwinde,
Shame burning brond-yrons in her hand did hold:
All three to each unlike, yet all made in one mould.

XXV
And after them a rude confused rout
Of persons flockt, whose names is hard to read:
Emongst them was sterne Strife, and Anger stout,
Unquiet Care, and fond Unthriftyhead,
Lewd Losse of Time, and Sorrow seeming dead,
Inconstant Chaunge, and false Disloyalty,
Consuming Riotise, and guilty Dread
Of Heavenly Vengeaunce, faint Infirmity,
Vile Poverty, and lastly Death with Infamy.

XXVI
There were full many moe like maladies,
Whose names and natures I note readen well;
So many moe, as there be phantasies
In wavering wemens witt, that none can tell,
Or paines in love, or punishments in hell;
All which disguized marcht in masking wise
About the chamber with that damozell,
And then returned, having marched thrise,
Into the inner rowme, from whence they first did rise.

XXVII
So soone as they were in, the dore streight way
Fast locked, driven with that stormy blast
Which first it opened; and bore all away.
Then the brave maid, which al this while was plast
In secret shade, and saw both first and last,
Issewed forth, and went unto the dore,
To enter in, but fownd it locked fast:
It vaine she thought with rigorous uprore
For to efforce, when charmes had closed it afore.

XXVIII
Where force might not availe, there sleights and art
She cast to use, both fitt for hard emprize:
Forthy from that same rowme not to depart

Till morrow next shee did her selfe avize,
When that same maske againe should forth arize.
The morrowe next appeard with joyous cheare,
Calling men to their daily exercize:
Then she, as morrow fresh, her selfe did reare
Out of her secret stand, that day for to outweare.

XXIX
All that day she outwore in wandering,
And gazing on that chambers ornament,
Till that againe the second evening
Her covered with her sable vestiment,
Wherewith the worlds faire beautie she hath blent:
Then, when the second watch was almost past,
That brasen dore flew open, and in went
Bold Britomart, as she had late forecast,
Nether of ydle showes nor of false charmes aghast.

XXX
So soone as she was entred, rownd about
Shee cast her eies, to see what was become
Of all those persons which she saw without:
But lo! they streight were vanisht all and some,
Ne living wight she saw in all that roome,
Save that same woefull lady, both whose hands
Were bounden fast, that did her ill become,
And her small waste girt rownd with yron bands,
Unto a brasen pillour, by the which stands.

XXXI
And her before, the vile enchaunter sate,
Figuring straunge characters of his art:
With living blood he those characters wrate,
Dreadfully dropping from her dying hart,
Seeming transfixed with a cruell dart;
And all perforce to make her him to love.
Ah! who can love the worker of her smart?
A thousand charmes he formerly did prove;
Yet thousand charmes not her stedfast hart remove.

XXXII
Soone as that virgin knight he saw in place,
His wicked bookes in hast he overthrew,
Not caring his long labours to deface;
And fiercely running to that lady trew,
A murdrous knife out of his pocket drew,
The which he thought, for villeinous despight,
In her tormented bodie to embre:
But the stout damzell to him leaping light,
His cursed hand withheld, and maistered his might.

XXXIII
From her, to whom his fury first he ment,
The wicked weapon rashly he did wrest,
And turning to herselfe his fell intent,
Unwares it strooke into her snowie chest,
That litle drops empurpled her faire brest.
Exceeding wroth therewith the virgin grew,
Albe the wound were nothing deepe imprest,
And fiercely forth her mortall blade she drew,
To give him the reward for such vile outrage dew.

XXXIV
So mightily she smote him, that to ground
He fell halfe dead; next stroke him should have slain,
Had not the lady, which by him stood bound,
Dernly unto her called to abstaine
From doing him to dy; for else her paine
Should be remedilesse, sith none but hee,
Which wrought it, could the same recure againe.
Therewith she stayd her hand, loth stayd to bee;
For life she him envyde, and long'd revenge to see:

XXXV
And to him said: 'Thou wicked man! whose meed
For so huge mischiefe and vile villany
Is death, or if that ought doe death exceed,
Be sure that nought may save thee from to dy,
But if that thou this dame doe presently
Restore unto her health and former state;
This doe and live, els dye undoubtedly.'
He, glad of life, that right willing to prolong his date:
Did yield him selfe right willing to prolong his date:

XXXVI
And rising up, gan streight to overlooke
Those cursed leaves, his charmes back to reverse;
Full dreadfull thinges out of that balefull booke
He red, and measur'd many a sad verse,
That horrour gan the virgins hart to perse,
And her faire locks up stared stiffe on end,
Hearing him those same bloody lynes reherse;
And all the while he red, she did extend
Her sword high over him, if ought he did offend.

XXXVII
Anon she gan perceive the house to quake,
And all the dores to rattle round about;
Yet all that did not her dismaied make,
Nor slack her threatfull hand for daungers dout,
But still with stedfast eye and courage stout
Abode, to weet what end would come of all.

At last that mightie chaine, which round about
Her tender waste was wound, adowne gan fall,
And that great brasen pillour broke in peeces small.

XXXVIII
The cruell steele, which thrild her dying hart,
Fell softly forth, as of his owne accord,
And the wyde wound, which lately did dispart
Her bleeding brest, and riven bowels gor'd,
Was closed up, as it had not beene bor'd,
And every part to safety full sownd,
As she were never hurt, was soone restor'd:
Tho, when she felt her selfe to be unbownd,
And perfect hole, prostrate she fell unto the grownd.

XXXIX
Before faire Britomart she fell prostrate,
Saying: 'Ah, noble knight! What worthy meede
Can wretched lady, quitt from wofull state,
Yield you in lieu of this your gracious deed?
Your vertue selfe her owne reward shall breed,
Even immortall prayse and glory wyde,
Which I, your vassall, by your prowesse freed,
Shall through the world make to be notifyde,
And goodly well advaunce, that goodly well was tryde.'

XL
But Britomart, uprearing her from grownd,
Said: 'Gentle dame, reward enough I weene,
For many labours more then I have found,
This, that in safetie now I have you seene,
And meane of your deliverance have beene:
Henceforth, faire lady, comfort to you take,
And put away remembraunce of late teene;
In sted thereof, know that your loving make
Hath no lesse griefe endured for your gentle sake.'

XLI
She much was cheard to heare him mentiond,
Whom of all living wightes she loved best.
Then laid the noble championesse strong hond
Upon th' enchaunter, which had her distrest
So sore, and with foule outrages opprest:
With that great chaine, wherewith not long ygoe
He bound that pitteous lady prisoner, now relest,
Himselfe she bound, more worthy to be so,
And captive with her led to wretchednesse and wo.

XLII
Returning back, those goodly rowmes, which erst
She saw so rich and royally arayd,

Now vanisht utterly and cleane subverst
She found, and all their glory quite decayd,
That sight of such a chaunge her much dismayd.
Thence forth descending to that perlous porch,
Those dreadfull flames she also found delayd,
And quenched quite, like a consumed torch,
That erst all entrers wont so cruelly to scorch.

XLIII
More easie issew now then entrance late
She found: for now that fained dreadfull flame,
Which chokt the porch of that enchaunted gate,
And passage bard to all that thither came,
Was vanisht quite, as it were not the same,
And gave her leave at pleasure forth to passe.
Th' enchaunter selfe, which all that fraud did frame,
To have efforst the love of that faire lasse,
Seeing his worke now wasted, deepe engrieved was.

XLIV
But when the victoresse arrived there
Where late she left the pensife Scudamore
With her own trusty squire, both full of feare,
Neither of them she found where she them lore:
Thereat her noble hart was stonisht sore ;
But most faire Amoret, whose gentle spright
Now gan to feede on hope, which she before
Conceived had, to see her own deare knight,
Being thereof beguyld, was fild with new affright.

XLV
But he, sad man, when he had long in drede
Awayted there for Britomarts returne,
Yet saw her not, nor signe of her good speed,
His expectation to despaire did turne,
Misdeeming sure that her those flames did burne ;
And therefore gan advize with her old squire,
Who her deare nourslings losse no lesse did mourne,
Thence to depart for further aide t' enquire:
Where let them wend at will, whilest here I doe respire.

Edmund Spenser – A Short Biography

One of the greatest of English poets, Edmund Spenser was born in East Smithfield, London, in 1552, though an exact date is not recorded.

As a boy, he was educated in London at the Merchant Taylors' School and later at Pembroke College, Cambridge.

As a young man, in 1578, the young Edmund was, for a short time, secretary to John Young, the Bishop of Rochester.

In 1579, he published The Shepheardes Calender, his first major work. The poem follows Colin Clout, a folk character originated by John Skelton, and depicts his life as a shepherd through the twelve months of the year.

It is also around this time that Edmund was married for the first time to Machabyas Childe. The union produced two children; Sylvanus and Katherine.

Edmund journeyed to Ireland in July 1580, in the service of the newly appointed Lord Deputy, Arthur Grey, 14th Baron Grey de Wilton. His time included the terrible massacre at the Siege of Smerwick, though this event seems to have settled his views somewhat on Ireland and the Irish. (The Siege of Smerwick took place at Ard na Caithne in 1580, during the Second Desmond Rebellion. A 400–500 strong force of Papal soldiers captured the town but were later forced to retreat to nearby Dún an Óir, where they were besieged by the English Army and eventually surrendered. On the orders of the English Commander most were then massacred).

When Lord Grey was recalled to England, Edmund stayed, having being appointed to several other official posts and lands in the Munster Plantation. Between 1587 and 1589, Spenser acquired his main estate at Kilcolman, near Doneraile in North Cork.

He later bought a second holding to the south, at Rennie, on a rock overlooking the river Blackwater but still in North Cork. Its ruins are still visible today. A short distance away grew a tree, locally known as "Spenser's Oak". Local legend has it that he penned some of The Faerie Queene under this very tree.

This epic poem, The Faerie Queene, is acknowledged as Edmund's masterpiece. The first three books were published in 1590, and a second set of three books were published in 1596. The original idea was for the poem to consist of twelve books. So although the version we publish here is all that he actually wrote it is still one of the longest, and most magnificent, poems in English literature.

The Faerie Queene is a work on several levels of allegory, including as praise of Queen Elizabeth I. The poem follows several knights in an examination of several virtues. In Spenser's "A Letter of the Authors," he states that the entire epic poem is "cloudily enwrapped in allegorical devises," and that the aim behind The Faerie Queene was to "fashion a gentleman or noble person in virtuous and gentle discipline."

On its publication Spenser travelled to London to publish and promote the work. In this endeavour he was successful enough to obtain a life pension of £50 a year from the Queen who did not give these out lightly.

Spenser used a verse form, now called the Spenserian stanza, in The Faerie Queene as well as several others poems. The stanza's main meter is iambic pentameter with a final line in iambic hexameter (having six stresses, known as an Alexandrine). He was also to use his own rhyme scheme for the sonnet. In a Spenserian sonnet, the last line of every stanza is linked with the first line of the next one.

Spenser was well read in classical literature and strove to emulate such Roman poets as Virgil and Ovid, whom he had studied during his schooling.

Indeed the reality is that Spenser, through his great talents, was able to move Poetry in a different direction. It led to him being called a Poet's Poet and brought rich admiration from Milton, Raleigh, Blake, Wordsworth, Keats, Byron, and Lord Tennyson, among others. John Milton in his Areopagitica called Spenser "our sage and serious poet . . . whom I dare be known to think a better teacher than Scotus or Aquinas".

He had hoped this praise and pension might lead to a position at Court but his next work antagonised the queen's principal secretary, Lord Burghley, through the inclusion of the satirical Mother Hubberd's Tale.

Spenser returned to Ireland and in 1591, Complaints, a collection of poems that voices complaints in mournful or mocking tones was published.

By 1594, Spenser's first wife, Machabyas, had died. Very soon he married Elizabeth Boyle, and to which he dedicated the sonnet sequence Amoretti. The marriage itself was celebrated in Epithalamion and the fruit of this relationship was a son, Peregrine.

In 1595, Spenser now published Amoretti and Epithalamion. The volume contains eighty-nine sonnets.

In the following year Spenser released Prothalamion, a wedding song written for the daughters of a duke, allegedly in hopes to gain favour in the court. More importantly he also wrote a prose pamphlet titled A View of the Present State of Ireland (A Veue of the Present State of Irelande). It was circulated in manuscript form due to its highly inflammatory content. Its main argument was that Ireland would never be totally 'pacified' by the English until its indigenous language and customs had been destroyed, if necessary by violence.

Spenser was a strong proponent of, and wished devoutly, that the Irish language should be eradicated, writing that if children learn Irish before English, "Soe that the speach being Irish, the hart must needes be Irishe; for out of the aboundance of the hart, the tonge speaketh".

He further discussed in the pamphlet future draconian plans to subjugate Ireland, after the most recent rising, led by Hugh O'Neill, having again shown the failure of previous efforts. The work is also a partial defence of Lord Arthur Grey de Wilton, with whom Spenser previously served and who deeply influenced Spenser's views on Ireland.

The goal of this piece was to show that Ireland was in great need of reform. Spenser believed that "Ireland is a diseased portion of the State, it must first be cured and reformed, before it could be in a position to appreciate the good sound laws and blessings of the nation". Spenser categorises the "evils" of the Irish people into three distinct categories: laws, customs, and religion. These three elements work together in creating the disruptive and degraded people. One example given in the work is the native law system called "Brehon Law" which trumps the established law given by the English monarchy. This system has its own court and way of dealing with troubles. It has been passed down through the generations and Spenser views this system as a native and backward custom which must be destroyed. (As an example the Brehon Law methods of dealing with murder by imposing an éraic, or fine, on the murderer's whole family particularly horrified the English, in whose Protestant view a murderer should die for his act.)

He pressed for a scorched earth policy in Ireland, noting that the destruction of crops and animals had been successful in crushing the Second Desmond Rebellion of which he was a part.

However in 1598, during the Nine Years War, Spenser was, ironically, driven from his home by the native Irish forces of Aodh Ó Néill. His castle at Kilcolman was burned.

In 1599, Spenser travelled to London, where he died on January 13th at the age of forty-six. According to Ben Jonson, in another and tragic irony it was "for want of bread".

Edmund Spenser's coffin was carried to his grave in Westminster Abbey by other poets, who threw many pens and pieces of poetry into his grave followed with many tears.

His second wife, Elizabeth, survived him and went on to remarry twice.

Spenser was called a Poets' Poet and was admired by John Milton, William Blake, William Wordsworth, John Keats, Lord Byron, and Alfred Lord Tennyson, among others. Walter Raleigh wrote a dedicatory poem to The Faerie Queene in 1590, in which he claims to admire and value Spenser's work more so than any other in the English language. John Milton in his Areopagitica called Spenser "our sage and serious poet . . . whom I dare be known to think a better teacher than Scotus or Aquinas".

It is praise indeed and clearly shows why Edmund Spenser is indeed part of the Pantheon of our greatest Poets.

Edmund Spenser – A Concise Bibliography

1569 - Jan van der Noodt's A theatre for Worldlings, including poems translated into English by Spenser from French sources.

1579 - The Shepheardes Calender, published under the pseudonym "Immerito".

1580 - Three proper, and wittie, familar letters

1590 - The Faerie Queene, Books I–III

1591 - Complaints, Containing sundrie small Poemes of the Worlds Vanitie

1592 - Axiochus, a translation of a pseudo-Platonic dialogue from the original Ancient Greek; attributed to "Edw: Spenser" but the attribution is uncertain

1592 - Daphnaïda. An Elegy upon the death of the noble and vertuous Douglas Howard, Daughter and heire of Henry Lord Howard, Viscount Byndon, and wife of Arthure Gorges Esquier

1595 - Amoretti and Epithalamion

1595 - Astrophel. A Pastorall Elegie vpon the death of the most Noble and valorous Knight, Sir Philip Sidney.

1595 - Colin Clouts Come home againe

1596 - Four Hymns (poem)|Fowre Hymnes dedicated from the court at Greenwich.

1596 - Prothalamion

1596 - The Faerie Queene, Books IV-VI

1598 - A Veue of the Present State of Irelande (Manuscript)

1599 - Babel, Empress of the East – a dedicatory poem prefaced to Lewes Lewkenor's The Commonwealth of Venice.

1609 - Two Cantos of Mutabilitie published together with a reprint of The Fairie Queene.

1611 - First folio edition of Spenser's collected works

1633 - A Veue of the Present State of Irelande, a prose treatise on the reformation of Ireland.

www.ingramcontent.com/pod-product-compliance
Lightning Source LLC
Chambersburg PA
CBHW061438040426
42450CB00007B/1117